The Flying Saucers are Real

Donald Keyhoe

1st WORLD
LIBRARY
Literary Society

The Flying Saucers are Real

Donald Keyhoe

© 1st World Library – Literary Society, 2004
PO Box 2211
Fairfield, IA 52556
www.1stworldlibrary.org
First Edition

LCCN: 2004091176

Softcover ISBN: 1-59540-622-0
Hardcover ISBN: 1-4218-0922-2
eBook ISBN: 1-59540-722-7

Purchase *"The Flying Saucers are Real"*
as a traditional bound book at:
www.1stWorldLibrary.org/purchase.asp?ISBN=1-59540-622-0

1st World Library Literary Society is a nonprofit
organization dedicated to promoting literacy by:

- Creating a free internet library accessible from any
computer worldwide.
- Hosting writing competitions and offering book
publishing scholarships.

The Flying Saucers are Real
contributed by the Mahaney Family
in support of
1st World Library Literary Society

To Helen,

with love

Donald E. Keyhoe, who relates here his investigation of the flying saucers, writes with twenty-five years of experience in observing aeronautical developments.

He is a graduate of the U.S. Naval Academy at Annapolis. He flew in active service with the Marine Corps, managed the tour of the historic plane in which Bennett and Byrd made their North Pole flight, was aide to Charles Lindbergh after the famous Paris flight, and was chief of information for the Aeronautics Branch, Department of Commerce.

Author's Note

ON APRIL 27, 1949, the U.S. Air Force stated:

"The mere existence of some yet unidentified flying objects necessitates a constant vigilance on the part of Project 'Saucer' personnel, and on the part of the civilian population.

"Answers have been - and will be - drawn from such factors as guided missile research activity, balloons, astronomical phenomena. . . . But there are still question marks.

"Possibilities that the saucers are foreign aircraft have also been considered. . . . But observations based on nuclear power plant research in this country label as 'highly improbable' the existence on Earth of engines small enough to have Powered the saucers.

"Intelligent life on Mars . . . is not impossible but is completely unproven. The possibility of intelligent life on the Planet Venus is not considered completely unreasonable by astronomers.

"The saucers are not jokes. Neither are they cause for alarm." [1]

On December 27, 1949, the Air Force denied the

existence of flying saucers.[2]

On December 30, 1949, the Air Force revealed part of a secret Project "Saucer" report to members of the press at Washington. The official report stated:

"It will never be possible to say with certainty that any individual did not see a space ship, an enemy missile, or some other object."

Discussing the motives of possible visitors from space, the report also stated:

"Such a civilization might observe that on Earth we now have atomic bombs and are fast developing rockets. In view of the past history of mankind, they should be

[1. Project "Saucer" Preliminary Study of Flying Saucers.

2. Air Force Press Release 629-49.'

alarmed. We should therefore expect at this time above all to behold such visitations."

(In its April 22 report, Project "Saucer" stated that space travel outside the solar system is almost a certainty.)

On February 22, 1950, the Air Force again denied the existence of flying saucers. On this same date, two saucers reported above Key West Naval Air Station were tracked by radar; they were described as maneuvering at high speed fifty miles above the earth. The Air Force refused to comment.

On March 9, 1950, a large metallic disk was pursued by F-51 and jet fighters and observed by scores of Air Force officers at Wright Field, Ohio. On March 18, an Air Force spokesman again denied that saucers exist and specifically stated that they were not American guided missiles or space-exploration devices.

I have carefully examined all Air Force saucer reports made in the last three years. For the past year, I have taken part in a special investigation of the flying-saucer riddle.

I believe that the Air Force statements, contradictory as they appear, are part of an intricate program to prepare America - and the world - for the secret of the disks.

CHAPTER I

IT WAS A strange assignment.

I picked up the telegram from my desk and read it a third time.

NEW YORK, N. Y., MAY 9, 1949

HAVE BEEN INVESTIGATING FLYING SAUCER MYSTERY. FIRST TIP HINTED GIGANTIC HOAX TO COVER UP OFFICIAL SECRET. BELIEVE IT MAY HAVE BEEN PLANTED TO HIDE REAL ANSWER. LOOKS LIKE TERRIFIC STORY. CAN YOU TAKE OVER WASHINGTON END?

KEN W. PURDY,
EDITOR, TRUE MAGAZINE

I glanced out at the Potomac, recalling the first saucer story. As a pilot, I'd been skeptical of flying disks. Then reports had begun to pour in from Air Force and airline pilots. Apparently alarmed, the Air Force had ordered fighters to pursue the fast-flying saucers. In one mysterious chase, a pilot had been killed, and his death was unexplained. That had been seventeen months ago. Since then, the whole flying-saucer riddle had been hidden behind a curtain of Air Force secrecy.

And now, an assignment from True magazine on flying saucers.

Twenty-four hours later, I was in Ken Purdy's office.

"I've had men on this for two months," he told me. "I might as well warn you, it's a tough story to crack."

"You think it's a Russian missile?" I asked him. "Or an Air Force secret?"

"We've had several answers. None of them stacks up. But I'm positive one was deliberately planted when they found we were checking."

He told me the whole story of the work that had been done by the staff of True and of the reports sent in by competent writers. The deeper he delved into the mystery, the tougher the assignment got. The more I learned about flying saucers, the less I knew.

"There's one angle I want rechecked," Purdy said.

"You've heard of the Mantell case?"

I nodded.

"O.K. Try to get the details of Mantell's radio report to Godman Tower. Before he was killed, he described the thing he was chasing - we know that much. Project 'Saucer' gave out a hint, but they've never released the transcript. Here's another lead. See if you can find anything about a secret picture, taken at Harmon Field, Newfoundland - it was around July 1947. I'll send you other ideas as I get them."

Before I left, Purdy wished me hick and told me that he would work in closest harmony with me.

"But watch out for fake tips," he said. "You'll probably run into some people at the Pentagon who'll talk to you 'off the record.' That handcuffs a writer. Look out they don't lead you into a blind alley. Even the Air Force statements and the Project 'Saucer' report contradict each other."

For six months, I worked with other investigators to solve the mystery of the disks. We checked a hundred sighting reports, frequently crossing the trail of Project "Saucer" teams and F.B.I. agents. Old records gave fantastic leads. So did Air Force plans for exploring space. Rocket experts, astronomers, Air Force officials and pilot gave us clues pointing to a startling solution. Many intelligent persons - including scientists - believe that the saucers contain spies from another planet.

When this first phase was ended, we were faced with a hard decision. We had uncovered important facts, We knew the saucers were real. If it was handled carefully, we believed the story would be in line with a secret Air Force policy.

It was finally decided to publish certain alternate conclusions. The Air Force was informed of True's intentions; no attempt was made to block publication.

In the January 1950 issue of True, I reported that we had reached the following conclusions:

1. The earth has been observed periodically by visitors from another planet.

2. This observation has increased markedly in the past two years.

"The only other possible explanation," I wrote, "is that, the saucers are extremely high-speed, long-range devices developed here on earth. Such an advance (which the Air Force has denied) would require an almost incredible leap in technical progress even for American scientists and designers."

Nation-wide press and radio comment followed the appearance of the article. This publicity was obviously greater than the Air Force had expected. Within twenty-four hours the Pentagon was deluged with telegrams, letters, and long-distance calls. Apparently fearing a panic, the Air Force hastily stated that flying-saucer reports - even those made by its own pilots and high-ranking officers - were mistakes or were caused by hysteria.[1]

But three days later, when it was plain that many Americans calmly accepted True's disclosures, the Air Force released a secret project "Saucer" file containing this significant statement:

"It will never be possible to say with certainty that any individual did not see a space ship, an enemy missile or other object."

In this same document there appears a confidential analysis of Air intelligence reports.[2] It is this summary that contains the official suggestion Of. space visitors' motives. After stating that such a civilization would obviously be far ahead of our own, the report adds:

"Since the acts of mankind most easily observed from a distance are A-bomb explosions, we should expect some relation to obtain between the time of the A-bomb explosions, the time at which the space ships are seen, and the time required for such ships to arrive from and return to home base."

(In a previous report, which alternately warned and reassured the public, the Air Force stated that space travel outside the solar system is almost a certainty.[3])

Since 1949 there has been a steady increase in saucer sightings. Most of them have been authentic reports, which Air Force denials cannot disprove. In January, mystery

[1. Air Force press release 629-49, December 27, 1949.

2. Air Force Project "Saucer" December 30, 1949.

3. Air Force report M-26-49, Preliminary Studies on Flying saucers, April 27, 1949.] disks were reported over Kentucky, Indiana, Texas, Pennsylvania, and several other states. On the Seattle Anchorage route, an air freighter was paced for five minutes by a night-flying saucer. When the pilots tried to close in, the strange craft zoomed at terrific speed. Later, the airline head reported that Intelligence officers had quizzed the pilots for hours.

"From their questions," he said, "I could tell they had a good idea of what the saucers are. One officer admitted they did, but he wouldn't say any more."

Another peculiar incident occurred at Tucson, Arizona,

on February 1. Just at dusk, a weird, fiery object raced westward over the city, astonishing hundreds in the streets below. The Tucson Daily Citizen ran the story next day with a double-banner headline:

FLYING SAUCER OVER TUCSON?

B-29 FAILS TO CATCH OBJECT

Flying saucer? Secret experimental plane? Or perhaps a scout craft from Mars? Certainly the strange aircraft that blazed a smoke trail over Tucson at dusk last night defies logical explanation. It was as mysti-fying to experienced pilots as to groundlings who have trouble in identifying conventional planes. Cannon-balling through the sky, some 30,000 feet aloft, was a fiery object shooting westward so fast it was impossible to gain any clear impression of its shape or size. . . . At what must have been top speed the object spewed out light colored smoke, but almost directly over Tucson it appeared to hover for a few seconds. The smoke puffed out an angry black and then be came lighter as the strange missile appeared to gain speed"

The radio operator in the Davis-Monthan air force base control tower contacted First Lt. Roy L. Jones, taking off for a cross-country flight in a B-29, and asked him to investigate. Jones revved up his swift aerial tanker and still the unknown aircraft steadily pulled away toward California. Dr. Edwin F. Carpenter, head of the University of Arizona depart-ment of astronomy, said he was certain that the object was not a meteor or other natural phenomenon. Switchboards Swamped Switch-boards at the Pima county sheriff's office and Tucson police station were jammed with inquiries. Hundreds saw the object. Tom Bailey, 1411 E. 10th Street,

Donald Keyhoe

thought it was a large airplane on fire. [A later check showed no planes missing.] He said it wavered from left to right as it passed over the mountains. Bailey also noticed that the craft appeared to slow perceptibly over Tucson. He said the smoke apparently came out in a thin, almost invisible stream, gaining substance within a few seconds.

This incident had an odd sequel the following day. Its significance was not lost on the Daily Citizen. It ran another front-page story, headlined:

WHAT DO YOU MEAN ONLY VAPOR TRAIL?

As though to prove itself blameless for tilting hundreds of Tucson heads skyward, the U.S. Air Force yesterday afternoon spent hours etching vapor trails through the skies over the city. The demonstration proved conclusively to the satisfaction of most that the strange path of dark smoke blazed across the evening sky at dusk Wednesday was no vapor trail and did not emanate from any conventional airplane.

The Wednesday night spectacle was entirely dissimilar. Then, heavy smoke boiled and swirled in a broad, dark ribbon fanning out at least a mile in width and stretching across the sky in a straight line. Since there was no proof as to what caused the strange predark manifestation, and because even expert witnesses were unable to explain the appearance, the matter remains a subject for interesting speculation.

There is strong evidence that this story was deliberately kept off the press wires. The Associated Press and other wire services in Washington had no report. Requests for details by Frank Edwards, Mutual newscaster, and other radio commentators ran into a blank wall. At the Pentagon I was told that the Air Force had no knowledge of the sighting or the vapor-trail maneuvers.

On February 22 two similar glowing objects were seen above Boca Chica Naval Air Station at Key West. A plane sent tip to investigate was hopelessly outdistanced; it was obvious the things were at a great height. Back at the station, radarmen tracked the objects as they hovered for a moment above Key West. They were found to be at least fifty miles above the earth. After a few seconds, they accelerated at high speed and streaked out of sight.

On the following day Commander Augusto Orrego, a Chilean naval officer, reported that saucers had flown above his antarctic base.

"During the bright antarctic night," be said, "we saw flying saucers, one above the other, turning at tremendous speeds. We have photographs to prove what we saw."

Early in March, Ken Purdy phoned the latest development in the investigation. He had just received a tip predicting a flurry of saucer publicity during March. It had come from an important source in Washington.

"You know what it probably means," he said. "The same thing we talked about last month. But why were we tipped off in advance?"

"It's one more piece in the pattern," I said. "If the tip's on the level, then they're stepping up the program."

Within three days, reports began to pour in - from Peru, Cuba, Mexico, Turkey, and other parts of the world. Then on March 9 a gleaming metallic disk was sighted over Dayton, Ohio. Observers at Vandalia Airport phoned Wright-Patterson Field. Scores of Air Force pilots and groundmen watched the disk, as fighters raced up in pursuit. The mysterious object streaked vertically skyward, hovered for a while miles above the earth, and then disappeared. A secret report was rushed to the Civil Aeronautics Authority in Washington, then turned over to Air Force Intelligence.

Soon after this Dr. Craig Hunter, director of a medical supply firm, reported a huge elliptical saucer flying at a low altitude in Pennsylvania. He described it as metallic, with a slotted outer rim and a rotating ring just inside. On top of this sighting, thousands of people at Farmington, New Mexico, watched a large formation of disks pass high above the city.

Throughout all these reports, the Air Force refused to admit the existence of flying saucers. On March 18 it flatly denied they were Air Force secret missiles or space-exploration devices.

Three days later, a Chicago and Southern airliner crew saw a fast-flying disk near Stuttgart, Arkansas. The circular craft, blinking a strange blue-white light, pulled up in an arc at terrific speed. The two pilots said they glimpsed lighted ports on the lower side as the saucer zoomed above them. The lights had a soft fluorescence, unlike anything they had seen.

There was one peculiar angle in the Arkansas incident. There was no apparent attempt to muzzle the two pilots, as in earlier airline cases. Instead, a United Press interview was quickly arranged, for nation-wide publication. In this wire story Captain Jack Adams and First Officer G. W. Anderson made two statements:

"We firmly believe that the flying saucer we saw over Arkansas was a secret experimental type aircraft - not a visitor from outer space. . .

"We know the Air Force has denied there is anything to this flying-saucer business, but we're both experienced pilots and we're not easily fooled."

The day after this story appeared, I was discussing it with an airline official in Washington.

"That's an odd thing," he said. "The Air Force could have persuaded those pilots - or the line president - to hush the thing up. It looks as if they wanted that story broadcast."

"You mean the whole thing was planted?"

"I won't say that, though it could have been. Probably they did see something. But they might have been told what to say about it."

"Any idea why?"

He looked at me sharply. "You and Purdy probably know the answer. At a guess, I'd say it might have been planned to offset that Navy commander's report - the one on the White Sands sightings."

The White Sands case had puzzled many skeptics, because the Pentagon had cleared the published report.

Donald Keyhoe

The author, Commander R. B. McLaughlin, was a regular Navy officer. As a Navy rocket expert, he had been stationed at the White Sands Rocket Proving Ground in New Mexico. In his published article he described three disk sightings at White Sands.

One of the disks, a huge elliptical craft, was tracked by scientists with precision instruments at five miles per second. That's 18,000 miles per hour. It was found to be flying fifty-six miles above the earth. Two other disks, smaller types, were watched from five observation posts on hills at the proving ground. Circling at incredible speed, the two disks paced an Army high-altitude rocket that had just been launched, then speeded up and swiftly outclimbed the projectile.

Commander McLaughlin's report, giving dates and factual details, was cleared by the Department of Defense. So was a later nation-wide broadcast.
Then the Air Force made its routine denial.

Why was McLaughlin, a regular Navy officer subject to security screening, permitted to give out this story? Was it an incredible slip-up? Or was it part of some carefully thought-out plan? I believe it was part of an elaborate program to prepare the American people for a dramatic disclosure.

For almost a year I have watched the behind-the-scenes maneuvers of those who guide this program. In the following chapters I have tried to show the strange developments in our search for the answer; the carefully misleading tips, the blind alleys we entered, the unexpected assistance, the confidential leads, and the stunning contradictions.

It has been a complicated jigsaw puzzle. Only by seeing all parts of this intricate picture can you begin to glimpse the reasons for this stubbornly hidden secret.

The official explanation may be imminent. When it is finally revealed, I believe the elaborate preparation - even the wide deceit involved - will be fully justified in the minds of the American people.

CHAPTER II

IT HAS BEEN over two years since the puzzling death of Captain Thomas Mantell.

Mantell died mysteriously in the skies south of Fort Knox. But before his radio went silent, he sent a strange message to Godman Air Force Base. The men who heard it will never forget it.

It was January 7, 1948.

Crowded into the Godman Field Tower, a group of Air Force officers stared up at the afternoon sky. For just an instant, something gleamed through the broken clouds south of the base.

High above the field, three P-51 fighters climbed with swift urgency. Heading south, they quickly vanished.

The clock in the tower read 2:45.

Colonel Guy Hix, the C.O., slowly put down his binoculars. If the thing was still there, the clouds now hid it. All they could do was wait.

The first alarm had come from Fort Knox, when Army M.P.'s had relayed a state police warning. A huge gleaming object had been seen in the sky, moving toward Godman Field. Hundreds of startled people had seen it at Madisonville, ninety miles away.

Thirty minutes later, it had zoomed up over the base.

Colonel Hix glanced around at the rest of the men in the tower. They all had a dazed look. Every man there had seen the thing, as it barreled south of the field. Even through the thin clouds, its intermittent red glow had hinted at some mysterious source of power. Something outside their understanding.

It was Woods, the exec, who had estimated its size. Hix shook his head. That was unbelievable. But something had hung over Godman Field for almost an hour. The C.O. turned quickly as the loud-speaker, tuned to the P-51's, suddenly came to life.

"Captain Mantell to Godman . . . Tower Mantell to Godman Tower . . ."

The flight leader's voice had a strained tone.

"I've sighted the thing!" he said. "It looks metallic - and it's tremendous in size!"

The C.O. and Woods stared at each other. No one spoke.

"The thing's starting to climb," Mantell said swiftly. "It's at twelve o'clock high, making half my speed. I'll try to close in."

In five minutes, Mantell reported again. The strange metallic object had speeded up, was now making 360 or more.

At 3:08, Mantell's wingman called in. Both he and the other pilot had seen the weird object. But Mantell had outclimbed them and was lost in the clouds.

Seven minutes dragged by. The men in the tower sweated out the silence. Then, at 3:15, Mantell made a hasty contact.

"It's still above me, making my speed or better. I'm going up to twenty thousand feet. If I'm no closer, I'll abandon chase."

It was his last report.

Minutes later, his fighter disintegrated with terrific force. The falling wreckage was scattered for thousands of feet.

When Mantell failed to answer the tower, one of his pilots began a search. Climbing to 33,000 feet, he flew a hundred miles to the south.

But the thing that lured Mantell to his death had vanished from the sky.

Ten days after Mantell was killed, I learned of a curious sequel to the Godman affair.

An A.P. account in the New York Times had caught my attention. The story, released at Fort Knox, admitted Mantell had died while chasing a flying saucer. Colonel Hix was quoted as having watched the object, which was still unidentified. But there was no mention of Mantell's radio messages - no hint of the thing's tremendous size.

Though I knew the lid was probably on, I went to the Pentagon. When the scare had first broken, in the summer of '47, I had talked with Captain Tom Brown, who was handling saucer inquiries. But by now Brown had been shifted, and no one in the Press Branch would admit knowing the details of the Mantell saucer chase.

"We just don't know the answer," a security officer told me.

"There's a rumor," I said, "it's a secret Air Force missile that sometimes goes out of control."

"Good God, man!" he exploded. "If it was, do you think we'd be ordering pilots to chase the damned things?"

"No - and I didn't say I believed it." I waited until he cooled down. "This order you mentioned - is it for all Air Force pilots, or special fighter units?"

"I didn't say it was a special order," he answered quickly. "All pilots have routine instructions to report unusual items."

"They had fighters alerted on the Coast, when the scare first broke," I reminded him. "Are those orders still in force?"

He shook his head. "No, not that I know of." After a moment he added, "All I can tell you is that the Air Force is still investigating. We honestly don't know the answer."

As I went out the Mall entrance, I ran into Jack Daly, one of Washington's veteran newsmen. Before the war,

Jack and I had done magazine pieces together, usually on Axis espionage and communist activity. I told him I was trying to find the answer to Mantell's death.

"You heard anything?" I asked him.

"Only what was in the A.P. story," said Jack. "But an I.N.S. man told me they had a saucer story from Columbus, Ohio - and it might have been the same one they saw at Fort Knox."

"I missed that. What was it?"

"They sighted the thing at the Air Force field outside of Columbus. It was around sundown, about two hours after that pilot was killed in Kentucky."

"Anybody chase it?" I asked.

"No. They didn't have time to take off, I guess. This I.N.S. guy said it was going like hell. Fast as a jet, anyway."

"Did he say what it looked like?"

"The Air Force boys said it was as big as a C-47," said Jack. "Maybe bigger. It had a reddish-orange exhaust streaming out behind. They could see it for miles."

"If you hear any more, let me know," I said. Jack promised he would.

"What do you think they are?" he asked me.

"It's got me stumped. Russia wouldn't be testing missiles over here. Anyway, I can't believe they've got anything like that. And I can't see the Air Force letting pilots get killed to hide something we've got."

One week later, I heard that a top-secret unit had been set up at Wright Field to investigate all saucer reports. When I called the Pentagon, they admitted this much, and that was all.

In the next few months, other flying-disk stories hit the front pages. Two Eastern Airline pilots reported a double-decked mystery ship sighted near Montgomery, Alabama. I learned of two other sightings, one over the Pacific Ocean and one in California. The second one, seen through field glasses, was described as rocket-shaped, as large as a B-29. There were also rumors of disks being tracked by radar, but it was almost a year before I confirmed these reports.

When Purdy wired me, early in May of '49, I had half forgotten the disks. It had been months since any important sightings had been reported. But his message quickly revived my curiosity. If he thought the subject was hot, I knew he must have reasons. When I walked into his office at 67 West 44th, Purdy stubbed out his cigarette and shook hands. He looked at me through his glasses for a moment. Then he said abruptly:

"You know anything about the disks?"

"If you mean what they are - no."

He motioned for me to sit down. Then he swiveled his chair around, his shoulders hunched forward, and frowned out the window.

"Have you seen the Post this week?"

I told him no.

"There's something damned queer going on. For fifteen months, Project 'Saucer' is buttoned up tight. Top secret. Then suddenly, Forrestal gets the Saturday Evening Post to run two articles, brushing the whole thing off. The first piece hits the stands - and then what happens?"

Purdy swung around, jabbed his finger at a document on. his desk.

"That same day, the Air Force rushes out this Project 'Saucer' report. It admits they haven't identified the disks in any important cases. They say it's still serious enough - wait a minute - "he thumbed through the stapled papers - " 'to require constant vigilance by Project "Saucer" personnel and the civilian population.'"

"You'd think the Post would make a public kick," I said.

"I don't mean it's an out-and-out denial," said Purdy. "It doesn't mention the Post - just contradicts it. In fact, the report contradicts itself. It looks as if they're trying to warn people and yet they're scared to say too much."

I looked at the title on the report: "A Digest of Preliminary Studies by the Air Materiel Command, Wright Field, Dayton, Ohio, on 'Flying Saucers.'"

"Have the papers caught it yet?" I asked Purdy.

"You mean its contradicting the Post?" He shook his head. "No, the Pentagon press release didn't get much space. How many editors would wade through a six-thousand-word government report? Even if they did, they'd have to compare it, item for item, with the Post piece."

"Who wrote the Post story?"

Purdy lit a cigarette and frowned out again at the skyscrapers.

"Sidney Shallett - and he's careful. He had Forrestal's backing. The Air Force flew him around, arranged interviews, supposedly gave him inside stuff. He spent two months on it. They O.K.'d his script, which practically says the saucers are bunk. Then they reneged on it."

"Maybe some top brass suddenly decided it was the wrong policy to brush it off," I suggested.

"Why the quick change?" demanded Purdy. "Let's say they sold the Post on covering up the truth, in the interests of security. It's possible, though I don't believe it. Or they could simply have fed them a fake story. Either Way, why did they rush this contradiction the minute the Post hit the stands?"

"Something serious happened," I said, "after the Post went to press."

"Yes, but what?" Purdy said impatiently. "That's what we've got to find out."

"Does Shallett's first piece mention Mantell's death?"

"Explains it perfectly. You know what Mantell was

chasing? The planet Venus!"

"That's the Post's answer?" I said, incredulously.

"It's what the Air Force contract astronomer told Shallett. I've checked with two astronomers here. They say that even when Venus is at full magnitude you can barely see it in the daytime even when you're looking for it. It was only half magnitude that day, so it was practically invisible."

"How'd the Air Force expect anybody to believe that answer?" I said.

Purdy shrugged. "They deny it was Venus in this report. But that's what they told Shallett - that all those Air Force officers, the pilots, the Kentucky state police, and several hundred people at Madisonville mistook Venus for a metallic disk several hundred feet in diameter."

"It's a wonder Shallett believed it."

"I don't think he did. He says if it wasn't Venus, it must have been a balloon."

"What's the Air Force answer?" I asked Purdy.

" Look in the report. They say whatever Mantell chased - they call it a 'mysterious object' - is still unidentified."

I glanced through the case report, on page five. It quoted Mantell's radio report that the thing was metallic and tremendous in size. Linked with the death of Mantell was the Lockbourne, Ohio, report, which tied in with what Jack Daly had told me, over a year before. I read the report:

"On the same day, about two hours later, a sky phenomenon was observed by several watchers over Lockbourne Air Force Base, Columbus, Ohio. It was described as 'round or oval, larger than a C-47, and traveling in level flight faster than 500 miles per hour.' The object was followed from the Lockbourne observation tower for more than 20 minutes. Observers said it glowed from white to amber, leaving an amber exhaust trail five times its own length. It made motions like an elevator and at one time appeared to touch the ground. No sound was heard. Finally, the object faded and lowered toward the horizon."

Purdy buzzed for his secretary, and she brought me a copy of the first Post article.

"You can get a copy of this Air Force report in Washington," Purdy told me. "This is the only one I have. But you'll find the same answer for most of the important cases - the sightings at Muroc Air Base, the airline pilots' reports, the disks Kenneth Arnold saw - they're all unidentified."

"I remember the Arnold case. That was the first sighting."

"You've got contacts in Washington," Purdy went on. "Start at the Pentagon first. They know we're working on it. Sam Boal, the first man on this job, was down there for a day or two."

"What did he find out?"

"Symington told him the saucers were bunk. Secretary Johnson admitted they had some pictures - we'd heard about a secret photograph taken at Harmon Field, Newfoundland. The tip said this saucer scared hell out of some pilots and Air Force men up there.

"A major took Boal to some Air Force colonel and Boal asked to see the pictures. The colonel said they didn't have any. He turned red when the major said Symington had told Boal about the pictures."

"Did Boal get to see them?" I said.

"No," grunted Purdy, "and I'll bet twenty bucks you won't, either. But try, anyway. And check on a rumor that they've tracked some disks with radar. One case was supposed to be at an Air Force base in Japan."

As I was leaving, Purdy gave me a summary of sighting reports.

"Some of these were published, some we dug up ourselves," he said. "We got some confidential stuff from airline pilots. It's pretty obvious the Air Force has tried to keep them quiet."

"All right," I said. "I'll get started. Maybe things aren't sewed up so tightly, now this report is out."

"We've found out some things about Project 'Saucer,' said Purdy. "Whether it's a cover-up or a real investigation, there's a lot of hush-hush business to it. They've got astronomers and astrophysicists working for them, also rocket expects, technical analysts, and Air Force Special Intelligence. We've been told they can call on any government agency for help - and I know they're using the F.B.I."

It was building up bigger than I had thought.

"If national security is involved," I told Purdy, "they can shut us up in a hurry."

"If they tell me so, O.K.," said Purdy. He added grimly, "But I think they're making a bad mistake. They probably think they're doing what's right. But the truth might come out the wrong way."

"It is possible," I thought, "that the saucers belong to Russia."

"If it turns out to be a Soviet missile, count me out," I said. "We'd have the Pentagon and the F.B.I. on our necks."

"All right, if that's the answer." He chuckled. "But you may be in for a jolt."

Donald Keyhoe

CHAPTER III

JUST THE idea of gigantic flying disks was incredible enough. It was almost as hard to believe that such missiles could have been developed without something leaking out. Yet we had produced the A-bomb in comparative secrecy, and I knew we were working on long-range guided missiles. There was already a plan for a three-thousand-mile test range. Our supersonic planes had hit around two thousand miles an hour. Our two-stage rockets had gone over two hundred miles high, according to reports. If an atomic engine had been secretly developed, it could explain the speed and range of the saucers.

But I kept coming back to Mantell's death and the Air Force orders for pilots to chase the saucers. If the disks were American missiles, that didn't jibe.

When I reached the lobby, I found it was ten after four. I caught a taxi and made the Congressional Limited with just one minute to spare. In the club car, I settled down to look at Purdy's summary.

Skipping through the pages, I saw several familiar cases. Here and there, Purdy had scrawled brief comments or suggestions. Beside the Eastern Airline report of a double-decked saucer, he had written:

"Check rumor same type seen over Holland about this date. Also, similar Philippine Islands report - date unknown."

I went back to the beginning. The first case listed was that of Kenneth Arnold, a Boise businessman, who had set off the saucer scare. Arnold was flying his private plane from Chehalis to Yakima, Washington, when he saw a bright flash on his wing.

Looking toward Mount Rainier, he saw nine gleaming disks outlined against the snow, each one about the size of a C-54.

"They flew close to the mountaintops, in a diagonal chainlike line," he said later. "It was as if they were linked together."

The disks appeared to be twenty to twenty-five miles away, he said, and moving at fantastic speed. Arnold's estimate was twelve hundred miles an hour.

"I watched them about three minutes," he said. "They were swerving in and out around the high mountain peaks. They were flat, like a pie pan, and so shiny they reflected the sun like a mirror. I never saw anything so fast."

The date was June 24, 1947.

On this same day there was another saucer report. which received very little notice. A Portland prospector named Fred Johnson, who was working up in the Cascade Mountains, spotted five or six disks banking in the sun. He watched them through his telescope several seconds. then he suddenly noticed that the compass hand on his special watch was weaving wildly from side to side. Johnson insisted he had not heard of the Arnold report, which was not broadcast until early evening.

Kenneth Arnold's story was generally received with amusement. Most Americans were unaware that the Pentagon had been receiving disk reports as early as January. The news and radio comments on Arnold's report brought several other incidents to light, which observers had kept to themselves for fear of ridicule.

At Oklahoma City, a private pilot told Air Force investigators he had seen a huge round object in the sky during the latter part of May. It was flying three times faster than a jet, he said, and without any sound. Citizens of Weiser, Idaho, described two strange fast-moving objects they had seen on June 12. The saucers were heading southeast, now and then dropping to a lower altitude, then swiftly climbing again. Several mysterious objects were reported flying at great speed near Spokane, just three days before Arnold's experience. And four days after his encounter, an Air Force pilot flying near Lake Meade, Nevada, was startled to see half a dozen saucers flash by his plane.

Even at this early point in the scare, official reports were contradicting each other. just after Arnold's story broke, the Air Force admitted it was checking on the mystery disks. On July 4 the Air Force stated that no further investigation was needed; it was all hallucination. That same day, Wright Field told the Associated Press that the Air Materiel Command was trying to find the answer.

The Fourth of July was a red-letter day in the

flying-saucer mystery. At Portland, Oregon, hundreds of citizens, including former Air Force pilots, police, harbor pilots, and deputy sheriffs, saw dozens of gleaming disks flying at high speed. The things; appeared to be at least forty thousand feet in the air - perhaps much higher.

That same day, disks were sighted at Seattle, Vancouver, and other northwest cities. The rapidly growing reports were met with mixed ridicule and alarm. One of the skeptical group was Captain E. J. Smith, of United Airlines.

"I'll believe them when I see them," he told airline employees, before taking off from Boise the afternoon of the Fourth.

Just about sunset, his airliner was flying over Emmett, Idaho, when Captain Smith and his copilot, Ralph Stevens, saw five queer objects in the sky ahead. Smith rang for the stewardess, Marty Morrow, and the three of them watched the saucers for several minutes. Then four more of the disks came into sight. Though it was impossible to tell their size, because their altitude was unknown, the crew was sure they were bigger than the plane they were in. After about ten minutes the disks disappeared.

The Air Force quickly denied having anything resembling the! Objects Captain Smith described.

" We have no experimental craft of that nature in Idaho - or anywhere else," an official said in Washington. "We're completely mystified."

The Navy said it had made an investigation, and had

no answers. There had been rumors that the disks were "souped-up" versions of the Navy's "Flying Flapjack," a twin-engined circular craft known technically as the XF-5-U-1. But the Navy insisted that only one model had been built, and that it was now out of service.

In Chicago, two astronomers spiked guesses that the disks might be meteors. Dr. Girard Kieuper, director of the University of Chicago observatory, said flatly that they couldn't be meteors.

"They're probably man-made," he told the A.P. Dr. Oliver Lee, director of Northwestern's observatory, agreed with Kieuper.

"The Army, Navy, and Air Force are working secretly on all sorts of things," he said. "Remember the A-bomb secrecy - and the radar signals to the moon."

As I went through Purdy's summary, I recalled my own reaction after the United Airlines report. After seeing the Pentagon comment, I had called up Captain Tom Brown, at Air Force Public Relations.

"Are you really taking this seriously?" I asked him.

"Well, we can't just ignore it," he said. "There are too many reliable pilots telling the same story - flat, round objects able to outmaneuver ordinary planes, and faster than anything we have. Too many stories tally."

I told him I'd heard that the Civil Air Patrol in Wisconsin and other states was starting a sky search.

"We've got a jet at Muroc, and six fighters standing by at Portland right now," Brown said.

"Armed?"

"I've no report on that. But I know some of them carry photographic equipment."

Two days later an airline pilot from the Coast told me that some fighters had been armed and the pilots ordered to bring down the disks if humanly possible. That same day, Wright Field admitted it was checking stories of disk-shaped missiles seen recently in the Pacific northwest and in Texas.

Following this was an A.P. story, dated July 7, quoting an unnamed Air Force official in Washington:

"The flying saucers may be one of three things:

"1. Solar reflection on low-hanging clouds. [A Washington scientist, asked for comment, said this was hardly possible.]

"2. Small meteors which break up, their crystals catching the rays of the sun. But it would seem that they would have been spotted falling and fragments would have been found.

"3. Icing conditions could have formed large hail-stones, and they might have flattened out and glided a bit, giving the impression of horizontal movement even though falling vertically."

By this time everyone was getting into the act.

"The disks are caused by the transmutation of atomic energy," said an anonymous scientist, supposed to be on the staff of California Tech. The college quickly denied it.

Dr. Vannevar Bush, world-famous scientist, and Dr. Merle Tuve, inventor of the proximity fuse, both declared they would know of any secret American missiles - and didn't.

At Syracuse, New York, Dr. Harry Steckel, Veterans Administration psychiatrist, scoffed at the suggestion of mass hysteria. "Too many sane people are seeing the things. The government is probably conducting some revolutionary experiments."

On July 8 more disks were reported. Out at Muroc Air Force Base, where top-secret planes and devices are tested, six fast-moving silvery-white saucers were seen by pilots and ground officers.

That afternoon the Air Force revealed it was working on a case involving a Navy rocket expert named C. T. Zohm. While on a secret Navy mission to New Mexico, in connection with rocket tests, Zohm had seen a bright silvery disk flying above the desert. He was crossing the desert with three other scientists when he saw the strange object flashing northward at an altitude of about ten thousand feet.

"I'm sure it was not a meteor," said Zohm. "It could have been a guided missile, but I never heard of anything like it."

By this time, saucer reports had come in from almost forty states. Alarm was increasing, and there were demands that radar be used to track the disks. The Air Force replied that there was not enough radar equipment to blanket the nation, but that its pilots were on the lookout for the saucers.

One report mentioned a curious report from Twin Falls, Idaho. The disk sighted there was said to have flown so low that the treetops whirled as if in a violent storm. Someone had phoned Purdy about a disk tracked by weather-balloon observers at Richmond, Virginia. There was another note on a sighting at Hickam Field, Honolulu, and two reports of unidentified objects seen near Anchorage, Alaska.

A typed list of world-wide sightings had been made up by the staff at True. It contained many cases that were new to me, reports from Paraguay, Belgium, Turkey, Holland, Germany, and the Scandinavian countries. At the bottom of this memo Purdy had written: "Keep checking on rumor that the Soviet has a Project Saucer, too. Could be planted."

From the mass of reports, John DuBarry, the aviation editor of True, had methodically worked out an average picture of the disks: "The general report is that they are round or oval (this could be an elliptical object seen end-on), metallic looking, very bright - either shining white or silvery colored. They can move at extremely high speed, hover, accelerate rapidly, and outmaneuver ordinary aircraft.

"The lights are usually seen singly - very few formations reported. They seem to have the same speed, acceleration, and ability to maneuver. In several cases, they have been able to evade Air Force planes in night encounters."

Going over the cases, I realized that Purdy and his staff had dug up at least fifty reports that had not appeared in the papers. (A few of these proved incorrect, but a check with the Air Force case reports released on December 30, 1949, showed that True's files contained all the important items.) These cases included sightings at eleven Air Force bases and fourteen American airports, reports from ships at sea, and a score of encounters by airline and private pilots.

Witnesses included Army, Navy, Marine Corps, and Air Force officers; state and city police; F.B.I. agents; weather observers, shipmasters, astronomers, and thousands of good solid American citizens. I learned later that many witnesses had been investigated by the F.B.I. to weed out crackpot reports.

I ended up badly puzzled. The evidence was more impressive than I had suspected. It was plain that many reports had been entirely suppressed, or at least kept out of the papers. There was something ominous about it. No matter what the answer, it was serious enough to be kept carefully hidden.

If it were a Soviet missile, I thought, God help us. They'd scooped up a lot of Nazi scientists and war secrets. And the Germans had been far ahead of us on guided missiles. But why would they give us a two-year warning, testing the things openly over America? It didn't make sense.

CHAPTER IV

I WENT to the Pentagon the next morning. I didn't expect to learn much, but I wanted to make sure we weren't tangling with security.

I'd worked with Al Scholin and Orville Splitt, in the magazine section of Public Relations, and I thought they'd tell me as much as anyone. When I walked in, I sprang it on them cold.

"What's the chance of seeing your Project 'Saucer' files?"

Al Scholin took it more or less dead-pan. Splitt looked at me a moment and then grinned.

"Don't tell me you believe the things are real?"

"Maybe," I said. "How about clearing me with Project 'Saucer'?"

Al shook his head. "It's still classified secret."

"'Look, Don," said Splitt, "why do you want to fool with that saucer business? There's nothing to it."

"'That's a big change from what the Air Force was saying; in 1947," I told him.

Donald Keyhoe

He shrugged that off. "The Air Force has spent two years checking into it. Everybody from Symington down will tell you the saucers are bunk."

"That's not what Project 'Saucer' says in that April report."

"That report was made up a long time ago," said Splitt. "They just got around to releasing it."

"Then they've got all the answers now?"

"They know there's nothing to it," Splitt repeated.

"In that case," I said, "Project 'Saucer' shouldn't object to my seeing their files and pictures."

"What pictures?"

"That one taken at Harmon Field, Newfoundland, for a starter."

"Oh, that thing," said Splitt. "It wasn't anything - just a shadow on a cloud. Somebody's been kidding you."

"If it's just a cloud shadow, why can't I see it?"

Splitt was getting a little nettled.

"Look, you know how long it takes to declassify stuff. They just haven't got around to it. Take my word for it, the flying saucers are bunk. I went around with Sid Shallett on some of his interviews. What he's got in the Post is the absolute gospel."

"It's funny about that April twenty-seventh report," I

said, "the way it contradicts the Post."

"I tell you that was an old report - "

"I wouldn't say that," Al Scholin put in. "The Air Force doesn't claim it has all the answers. But they've proved a lot of the reports were hoaxes or mistakes."

"Just the same," I said, "the Air Force is on record, as of April twenty-seventh, that it's serious enough for everybody to be vigilant. And they admit most of the things, in the important cases, are still unidentified. Including the saucer Mantell was chasing."

"That business at Godman Field was some kind of hallucination," insisted Splitt.

"I suppose all those pilots and Godman Field officers were hypnotized? Not to mention several thousand people at Madisonville and Fort Knox?"

"Take it easy, you guys," said Al Scholin. "You've both got a right to your opinions."

"Oh, sure," said Splitt. He looked at me, with his grin back. "I don't care if you think they're men from Mars."

"Let's not go off the deep end," I said. "Tell me this: Did Shallett get to see any secret files at Wright Field?"

"Absolutely not."

"Then he had to take the Air Force word for everything?"

"Not entirely. We set up some interviews for him."

"One more thing - and don't get mad. If it's all bunk, why haven't they closed Project 'Saucer'?"

"How do I know? Probably no one wants to take the responsibility."

"Then somebody high up must not think it's bunk," I said.

Splitt laughed. "Have it your own way."

Before I left, I told them I was working with True.

"I want to be on record," I said, "as having told you this. If there's any security involved - if you tell me it's something you're working on - naturally I'll lay off."

Al Scholin said emphatically, "It's not an Air Force device, if that's what you mean."

"Some people think it's Russian."

"If it is, I don't know it," said Al, "and neither does the Air Force."

After I left the magazine section, I tried several officers I knew. Two of them agreed with Splitt. The third didn't.

"I've been told it's all bunk," he said, "but you get the feeling they've trying to convince themselves. They act like people near a haunted house. They'll swear it isn't haunted - but they won't go near it."

Later, I asked a security major for a copy of the Project "Saucer" report.

"We're out of copies right now," he said. "I'll send you one next week."

I asked him bluntly what he thought the saucers were.

"I doubt if anybody has the full answer," he said seriously. "There's been some hysteria - also a few mistakes. But many reports have been made by reliable pilots, including our own. You can't laugh those off."

As I drove home, I thought over what I'd heard. All I had learned was that the Air Force seemed divided. But that could be a smoke screen. In less than twenty-four hours, I received my first suspicious tip. It was about ten A.M. when my phone rang.

"Mr. Keyhoe? This is John Steele," said the voice at the other end. (Because of the peculiar role he played, then and later, I have not used his real name.) "I'm a former Air Force Intelligence officer. I was in the European theater during the war."

I waited. He hesitated a moment.

"I heard you're working on the flying-saucer problem," he said quickly. "I may have some information that would interest you."

"Mind telling me who told you I was on it?" I asked.

"No one, directly. I just happened to hear it mentioned at the Press Club. Frankly, I've been curious about the flying saucers ever since '45."

That startled me, but I didn't tell him so.

"Do you have any idea what they are?" Mr. Steele said.

"No, I've just begun checking. But I'd be glad to hear what you've got."

"I may be way off," said Steele. "But I've always wondered about the 'foo fighters' our pilots saw over Europe near the end of the war."

I thought for a second. "Wasn't that some kind of antiaircraft missile fired from the ground?"

"No. Intelligence never did get any real answer, so far as I know. They were some kind of circular gadgets, and they actually chased our planes a number of times. We thought they were something the Nazis had invented - and I still think so."

"Then who's launching them now?"

"Well, it's obviously either Russia or us. If it is the Soviet - well, that's what's worried me. I don't think it should be treated like a joke, the way some people in the Pentagon take it."

I stared at the phone, trying to figure him out.

"I'd like to talk it over with you," I said. "Maybe you've got something."

"I've given you about all I know," Steele answered. "There was an Intelligence report you might try to see - the Eighth Air Force files should have it."

"Wait a minute," I said. "Give me your number, in case I find anything."

He gave it to me without apparent hesitation. I thanked him and hung up, still wondering.

If it was an attempt at a plant, it was certainly crude. The mention of his former Air Force connection would be enough to arouse suspicion, unless he counted on his apparent frankness to offset it.

And what about the Press Club angle? That would indicate Steele was a newspaperman. Could this be merely an attempt to pump me and get a lead on True's investigation? But that would be just as crude as the other idea. Of course, he might be sincere. But regardless of his motives, it looked bad. Arid who had told him about me?

I thought about that for a minute. Then I picked up the phone and dialed Jack Daly's number.

"Jack, do you know anyone named John Steele?" I asked him. "I think he's a newspaperman."

"Nobody I know," said Jack. "Why, what's up?"

I explained, and added, "I thought maybe you knew him, and he'd heard about it from you."

"Hell, no," said Jack. "You ought to know I wouldn't leak any tip like that."

"It wouldn't be a tip - I don't know anything about this deal yet. By the way, when you were on the Star did you handle anything on 'foo fighters'?"

"No, that was after I left there. Bill Shippen would have covered that, anyway."

I told him I would look it up in the Star's morgue. Jack said he would meet me there at three o'clock; in the meantime he would see what he could find out about Steele.

Jack was a little late, and I went over the Star's file on the foo fighters. Most of the facts were covered in a story dated July 6, 1947, which had been inspired by the outbreak of the saucer scare. I copied it for later use:

During the latter part of World War Two, fighter pilots in England were convinced that Hitler had a new secret weapon. Yanks dubbed these devices "foo fighters" or "Kraut fireballs." One of the Air Force Intelligence men now assigned to check on the saucer scare was an officer who investigated statements of military airmen that circular foo fighters were seen over Europe and also on the bombing route to Japan. It was reported that Intelligence officers have never obtained satis- factory explanation of reports of flying silver balls and disks over Nazi-occupied Europe in the winter of 1944-45. Later, crews of B-29'S on bombing runs to Japan reported seeing somewhat similar objects.

In Europe, some foo fighters danced just off the Allied fighters' wingtips and played tag with them in power dives. Others appeared in precise formations and on one occasion a whole bomber crew saw about 15 following at a distance, their strange glow flashing on and off. One foo fighter chased Lieutenant Meiers of Chicago some 20 miles down the Rhine Valley, at 300 m.p.h., an A.P. war correspondent reported.

Intelligence officers believed at that time that the balls might be radar-controlled objects sent up to foul ignition systems or baffle Allied radar networks. There is no explanation of their appearance here, unless the objects could have been imported for secret tests in this country.

I read the last paragraph twice. This looked like a strong lead to the answer, in spite of the Air Force denials. There was another, less pleasant possibility. The Russians could have seized the device and developed it secretly, using Nazi scientists to help them. Perhaps the Nazis had been close to an atomic engine, even if they did fail to produce the bomb.

Jack Daly came in while I was reading the story again.

"I got the dope on Steele," he said. "He does pieces for a small syndicate, and I found out he was in the Air Force. I think he was a captain. People who know him say he's O.K. - a straight shooter."

"That still wouldn't keep him from giving me a fake tip, if somebody told him it was the right thing to do."

"Maybe not," said Jack, "but why would they want to plant this foo-fighter idea?"

I showed him the clipping. He read it over and shook his head.

"That's a lot different from disks three hundred feet in diameter."

"If we got the principle - or Russia did-building big ones might not be too hard."

"I still can't swallow it," said Jack. "These things have been seen all over the world. How could they control them that far away - and be sure they wouldn't crash, where somebody could get a look and dope out the secret?"

We argued it back and forth without getting anywhere.

"I'd give a lot to know Steele's angle," I said. "If you hear anything more on him, give me a buzz."

Jack nodded. "I'll see what I can do. But I can't dig too hard, or he'll hear about it."

On the way out, I found a phone booth and called Splitt.

"Foo fighters?" he said. "Sure, I remember those stories. You think those are your flying saucers?"

I could hear him snicker.

"Just checking angles," I said. "Didn't the Eighth Air Force investigate the foo fighters?"

"Yes, and they found nothing to back up the pilots' yarns. just war nerves, apparently."

"How about a look at the Intelligence report?" I asked.

"Wait a minute." Splitt was gone for twice that time, then he carne back. "Sorry, it's classified."

"If all this stuff is bunk, why keep the lid on it?" I demanded. I was getting sore again.

"Look, Don," said Splitt, "I don't make the rules."

"Sure, I know - sorry," I said. I had a notion to ask him if he knew John Steele, but hung up instead. There was no use in banging my head against the Air Force wall.

The next day I decided to analyze the Mantell case from beginning to end. It looked like the key to one angle: the question of an Air Force secret missile. Unless there was some slip-up, so that Mantell and his pilots had been ordered to chase the disk by mistake, then it would be cold murder.

I couldn't believe any Air Force officer would give such an order, no matter how tremendous the secret to be hidden.

But I was going to find out, if possible.

CHAPTER V

FOR MORE than two weeks, I checked on the Godman Field tragedy. One fact stood out at the start: The death of Mantell had had a profound effect on many in the Air Force. A dozen times I was told:

"I thought the saucers were a joke-until Mantell was killed chasing that thing at Fort Knox."

Many ranking officers who had laughed at the saucer scare stopped scoffing. One of these was General Sory Smith, now Deputy Director of Air Force Public Relations. Later in my investigation, General Smith told me:

"It was the Mantell case that got me. I knew Tommy Mantell. Very well - also Colonel Hix, the C.O. at Godman. I knew they were both intelligent men - not the kind to be imagining things."

For fifteen months, the Air Force kept a tight-lipped silence. Meantime, rumors began to spread. One report said that Mantell had been shot, his body riddled with bullets; his P-51, also riddled, had simply disintegrated. Another rumor reported Mantell as having been killed by some mysterious force; this same force had also destroyed his fighter. The Air Force, the rumors said, had covered up the truth by telling Mantell's family he had blacked out from lack of oxygen.

Checking the last angle, I found that this was the explanation given to Mantell's mother, just after his death, she was told by Standiford Field officers that he had flown too high in chasing the strange object.

Shallet, in the Saturday Evening Post articles, described Project "Saucer's" reconstruction of the case. Mantell was said to have climbed up to 25,000 feet, despite his firm decision to end the chase at 20,000, since he carried no oxygen. Around 25,000 feet, Shallett quoted the Air Force investigators, Mantell must have lost consciousness. After this, his pilotless plane climbed on up to some 30,000 feet, then dived. Between 20,000 and 10,000 feet, Shallett suggested, the P-51 began to disintegrate, obviously from excessive speed. The gleaming object that hypnotized Mantell into this fatal climb was, Shallett said, either the planet Venus or a Navy cosmic-ray research balloon.

The Air Force Project "Saucer" report of April 27, 1949, released just after the first Post article, makes these statements:

"Five minutes after Mantell disappeared from his formation, the two remaining planes returned to Godman. A few minutes later, one resumed the search, covering territory 100 miles to the south as high as 33,000 feet, but found nothing.

"Subsequent investigation revealed that Mantell had probably blacked out at 20,000 feet from lack of oxygen and had died of suffocation before the crash.

"The mysterious object which the flyer chased to his death was first identified as the Planet Venus. However, further probing showed the elevation and azimuth readings of Venus and the object at specified time intervals did not coincide.

"It is still considered 'Unidentified.'

The Venus explanation, even though now denied, puzzled me. It was plain that the Air Force had seriously considered offering it as the answer then abandoned it. Apparently someone had got his signals mixed and let Shallett use the discarded answer. And for some unknown reason, the Air Force had found it imperative to deny the Venus story at once.

In these first weeks of checking, I had run onto the Venus explanation in other cases. Several Air Force officers repeated it so quickly that it had the sound of a stock alibi. But in the daytime cases this was almost ridiculous.

I knew of a few instances in World War II when bomber crews and antiaircraft gunners had loosed a few bursts at Venus. But this was mostly at night, when the planet was at peak brilliance. And more than one gunner later admitted firing to relieve long hours of boredom. Since enemy planes did not carry lights, there was no authentic case, to my knowledge, where plane or ground gunners actually believed Venus was an enemy aircraft.

Checking the astronomer's report, I read over the concluding statement:

"It simply could not have been Venus. They must have

been desperate even to suggest it in the first place." Months later, in the secret Project "Saucer" report released December 30, 1949, I found official confirmation of this astronomer's opinions. Since it has a peculiar bearing on the Mantell case, I am quoting it now:

When Venus is at its greatest brilliance, it is possible to see it during daytime when one knows exactly where to look. But on January 7, 1948, Venus was less than half as bright as its peak brilliance. However, under exceptionally good atmospheric conditions, and with the eye shielded from direct rays of the sun, Venus might be seen as an exceedingly tiny bright point of light. However, the chances of looking at just the right spot are very few.

It has been unofficially reported that the object was a Navy cosmic-ray research balloon. If this can be established, it Is to be preferred as an explanation. However, if one accepts the assumption that reports from various other localities refer to the same object, any such device must have been a good many miles high - 25 to 50 - in order to have been seen clearly, almost simultaneously, from places 175 miles apart.

If all reports were of a single object, in the knowledge of this investigator no man-made object could have been large enough and far enough away for the approximate simultaneous sightings. It is most unlikely, however, that so many separated persons should at that time have chanced on Venus in the daylight sky. It seems therefore much more probable that more than one object was involved.

The sighting might have included two or more

balloons (or aircraft) or they might have included Venus and balloons. For reasons given above, the latter explanation seems more likely.

Two things stand out in his report:

1. The obvious determination to fit some explanation, no matter how farfetched, to the Mantell sighting.

2. The impossibility that Venus - a tiny point of light, seen only with difficulty - was the tremendous metallic object described by Mantell and seen by Godman Field officers.

With Venus eliminated, I went to work on the balloon theory. Since I had been a balloon pilot before learning to fly planes, this was fairly familiar ground.

Shallett's alternate theory that Mantell had chased a Navy research balloon was widely repeated by readers unfamiliar with balloon operation. Few thought to check the speeds, heights, and distances involved.

Cosmic-ray research balloons are not powered; they are set free to drift with the wind. This particular Navy type is released at a base near Minneapolis. The gas bag is filled with only a small per cent of its helium capacity before the take-off.

In a routine flight, the balloon ascends rapidly to a very high altitude-as high as 100,000 feet. By this time the gas bag has swelled to full size, about 100 feet high and 70 feet in diameter. At a set time, a device releases the case of instruments under the balloon. The instruments descend by parachute, and the balloon, rising quickly, explodes from the sudden expansion.

Occasionally a balloon starts leaking, and it then remains relatively low. At first glance, this might seem the answer to the Kentucky sightings. If the balloon were low enough, it would loom up as a large circular object, as seen from directly below. Some witnesses might estimate its diameter as 250 feet or more, instead of its actual 70 feet. But this failure to recognize a balloon would require incredibly poor vision on the part of trained observers - state police, Army M.P.'s, the Godman Field officers, Mantell and his pilots.

Captain Mantell was a wartime pilot, with over three thousand hours in the air. He was trained to identify a distant enemy plane in a split second. His vision was perfect, and so was that of his pilots. In broad daylight they could not fail to recognize a balloon during their thirty-minute chase.

Colonel Hix and the other Godman officers watched the object with high-powered glasses for long periods. It is incredible that they would not identify it as a balloon.

Before its appearance over Godman Field, the leaking balloon would have drifted, at a low altitude, over several hundred miles. (A leak large enough to bring it down from high altitude would have caused it to land and be found.) Drifting at a low altitude, it would have been seen by several hundred thousand people, at the very least. Many would have reported it as a balloon. But even if this angle is ignored it still could not possibly have been a balloon at low altitude. The fast flight from Madisonville, the abrupt stop and hour-long hovering at Godman Field, the quick bursts of speed Mantell reported make it impossible. To fly the go miles from Madisonville to Fort Knox in 30 minutes, a balloon would require a wind of 180 m.p.h. After traveling at this hurricane speed, it would then have had to come to a dead stop above Godman Field. As the P-51's approached, it would have had to speed tip again to 180, then to more than 360 to keep ahead of Mantell.

The three fighter pilots chased the mysterious object for half an hour. (I have several times chased balloons with a plane, overtaking them in seconds.) In a straight chase, Mantell would have been closing in at 360; the tail wind acting on his fighter would nullify the balloon's forward drift.

But even if you accept these improbable factors, there is one final fact that nullifies the balloon explanation. The strange object had disappeared when Mantell's wingman searched the sky, just after the leader's death. If it had been a balloon held stationary for an hour at a high altitude, and glowing brightly enough to be seen through clouds, it would have remained visible in the same general position. Seen from 33,000 feet, it would have been even brighter, because of the clearer air.

But the mysterious object had completely vanished in those few minutes. A search covering a hundred miles failed to reveal a trace.

Whether at a high or low altitude, a balloon could not have escaped the pilot's eyes. It would also have continued to be seen at Godman Field and other points, through occasional breaks in the clouds.

I pointed out these facts to one Air Force officer at the Pentagon. Next day he phoned me:

"I figured it out. The timing device went off and the balloon exploded. That's why the pilot didn't see it."

"It's an odd coincidence," I said, "that it exploded in those five minutes after Mantell's last report."

"Even so, it's obviously the answer," he said.

Checking on this angle, I found:

1. No one in the Kentucky area had reported a descending parachute.

2. No cosmic-ray research instrument case or parachute was found in the area.

3. No instruments were returned to the Navy from this region. And all balloons and instruments released at that time were fully accounted for.

Even if it had been a balloon, it would not explain the later January 7th reports - the simultaneous sightings mentioned by Professor Hynek in the Project "Saucer" report. This includes the thing seen at Lockbourne Air Force Base two hours after Mantell's death.

Obviously, the saucer seen flying at 500 m.p.h. over Lockbourne Field could not have been a balloon. Even if there had been several balloons in this area (and there were not, by official record), they could not have covered the courses reported. In some cases, they would have been flying against the wind, at terrific speed.

Then what was the mysterious object? And what killed Mantell?

Both the Air Force and the Post articles speculate that Mantell carelessly let himself black out.

Since some explanation had to be given, this might seem a good answer. But Mantell was known for coolheaded judgment. As a wartime pilot, he was familiar with signs of anoxia (oxygen starvation). That he knew his tolerance for altitude is proved by his firmly declared intention to abandon the chase at 20,000 feet, since he had no oxygen equipment.

Mantell had his altimeter to warn him. From experience, he would recognize the first vague blurring, narrowing of vision, and other signs of anoxia. Despite this, the "blackout" explanation was accepted as plausible by many Americans.

While investigating the Mantell case, I talked with several pilots and aeronautical engineers. Several questioned that a P-51 starting a dive from 20,000 feet would have disintegrated so thoroughly.

"From thirty thousand feet, yes," said one engineer. "If the idea was to explain it away, I'd pick a high altitude to start from. But a pilotless plane doesn't necessarily dive, as you know.

"It might slip off and spin, or spiral down, and a few have even landed themselves. Also, if the plane started down from twenty thousand, the pilot wouldn't be too far blacked out. The odds are he'd come to when he got into thicker air - admitting he did blur out, which is only an Air Force guess. I don't see why they're so positive Mantell died before he hit the ground - unless they know something we don't."

One of the pilot group put it more bluntly.

"It looks like a cover-up to me. I think Mantell did just what he said he would - close in on the thing. I think he either collided with it, or more likely they knocked him out of the air. They'd think he was trying to bring them down, barging in like that."

Even if you accept the blackout answer, it still does not explain what Mantell was chasing. it is possible that, excited by the huge, mysterious object, he recklessly climbed beyond the danger level, though such an act was completely at odds with his character.

But the identity of the thing remains - officially - a mystery. If it was some weird experimental craft or a guided missile, then whose was it? Air Force officers had repeatedly told me they had no such device. General Carl Touhy Spaatz, former Air Force chief, had publicly insisted that no such weapon had been developed in his regime. Secretary Symington and General Hoyt Vandenberg, present Air Force chief, had been equally emphatic. Of course, official denials could be expected if it were a top-level secret. But if it were a secret device, would it be tested so publicly that thousands would see it?

If it were an Air Force device, then I could see only one answer for the Godman Field incident: The thing was such a closely guarded secret that even Colonel Hix hadn't known. That would mean that most or all Air Force Base C.O.'s were also in ignorance of the secret device.

Could it be a Navy experiment, kept secret from the Air Force?

I did a little checking.

Admiral Calvin Bolster, chief of aeronautics research experimental craft, was an Annapolis classmate of mine. So was Captain Delmer S. Fahrney, head of the Navy guided-missile program. Fahrney was at Point Mugu, missile-testing base in California, and I wasn't able to see him. But I knew him as a careful, conscientious officer; I can't believe he would let such a device, piloted or not, hover over an Air Force base with no warning to its C.O.

I saw Admiral Bolster. His denial seemed genuine; unless he'd got to be a dead-pan poker player since our earlier days, I was sure he was telling the truth.

The only other alternate was Russia. It was incredible that they would develop such a device and then expose it to the gaze of U.S. Air Force officers. It could be photographed, its speed and maneuverability checked; it might crash, or antiaircraft fire might bring it down, The secret might be lost in one such test flight.

There was one other explanation: The thing was not intended to be seen; it had got out of control. In this event; the long hovering period at Godman Field was caused by the need for repairs inside the flying saucer, or repairs to remote-control apparatus.

If it were Air Force or Navy, that would explain official concern; even if completely free of negligence, the service responsible would be blamed for Mantell's death. If it were Russian, the Air Force would of course try to conceal the fact for fear of public hysteria.

But if the device was American, it meant that Project "Saucer" was a cover-up unit. While pretending to investigate, it would actually hush up reports, make false explanations, and safeguard the secret in every possible way. Also, the reported order for Air Force pilots to pursue the disks would have to be a fake. Instead, there would be a secret order telling them to avoid strange objects in the sky.

By the time I finished my check-up, I was sure of one thing: This particular saucer had been real.

I was almost positive of one other point-that the thing had been over 30 miles high during part of its flight. I found that after Mantell's death it was reported simultaneously from Madisonville, Elizabethtown, and Lexington - over a distance of 175 miles. (Professor Hynek's analysis later confirmed this.)

How low it had been while hovering over Godman, and during Mantell's chase, there was no way to determine. But all the evidence pointed to a swift ascent after Mantell's last report.

Had Mantell told Godman Tower more than the Air Force admitted? I went back to the Pentagon and asked for a full transcript of the flight leader's radio messages. I got a quick turn-down. The reports, I was told, were still classified as secret. Requests for pictures of the P-51 wreckage, and for a report on the condition of Mantell's body, also drew a blank. I had heard that some photographs were taken of the Godman Field saucer from outside the tower. But the Air Force denied knowledge of any such pictures.

Puzzling over the riddle, I remembered John Steele,

the former Intelligence captain. If by any chance he was a plant, it would be interesting to suggest the various answers and watch his reaction. When I phoned him to suggest luncheon, Steele accepted at once. We met at the Occidental, on Pennsylvania Avenue. Steele was younger than I had expected - not over twenty-five. He was a tall man, with a crew haircut and the build of a football player. Looking at him the first time, I expected a certain breeziness. instead, he was almost solemn.

"I owe you an apology," he said in a careful voice afterwe'd ordered. "You probably know I'm a syndicate writer?"

I wondered if he'd found out Jack Daly was checking on him.

"When you mentioned the Press Club," I said, "I gathered you were in the business."

"I'm afraid you thought I was fishing for a lead." Steele looked at me earnestly. "I'm not working on the story - I'm tied up on other stuff."

"Forget it," I told him.

He seemed anxious to reassure me. "I'd been worried for some time about the saucers. I called you that night on an impulse."

"Glad you did," I said. "I need every tip I can get."

"Did it help you any?"

"Yes, though it still doesn't fit together. But I can tell

you this: The saucers are real, or at least one of them."

"Which one?"

"The thing Captain Mantell was chasing near Fort Knox, before he died."

"Oh, that one." Steele looked down at the roll he was buttering. "I thought that case was fully explained. Wasn't he chasing a balloon?"

"The Air Force says it's still unidentified." I told him what I had learned. "Apparently you're right - it's either an American or a Soviet missile."

"After what you've told me," said Steele, "I can't believe it's ours. It must be Russian."

"They'd be pretty stupid to test it over here."

"You said it was probably out of control."

"That particular one, maybe. But there have been several hundred seen over here. If they found their controls were haywire, they wouldn't keep testing the things until they'd corrected that."

The waiter came with the soup, and Steele was silent until he left.

"I still can't believe it's our weapon," he said slowly. "They wouldn't have Air Force pilots alerted to chase the things. And I happen to how they do."

"There's something queer about this missile angle," I said. "That saucer was seen at the same time by people a hundred and seventy-five miles apart. To be that high in the sky, and still look more than two hundred and fifty feet in diameter, it must have been enormous."

Steele didn't answer for a moment.

"Obviously, that was an illusion," he finally answered. "I'd discount those estimates."

"Even Mantell's? And the Godman Field officers'?"

"Not knowing the thing's height, how could they judge accurately?"

"To be seen at points that far apart, it had to be over thirty miles high," I told him. "It would have to be huge to show up at all."

He shook his head. "I can't believe those reports are right. It must have been sighted at different times."

I let it drop.

"What are you working on now?" Steele asked, after a minute or two.

I said I hadn't decided. Actually, I planned a trip to the coast, to interview pilots who had sighted flying disks.

"What would you do if you found it wasn't a Soviet missile?" said Steele. He sounded almost too casual.

"If security was involved, I'd keep still. But the Air Force and the Navy swear they haven't any such things."

Steele looked at me thoughtfully.

"You know, True might force something into the open that would be better left secret." He smiled ironically. "I realize that sounds peculiar, since I suggested the Russian angle. But if it isn't Russian - though I still think it is - then we have nothing to worry about."

I was almost sure now that he was a plant. During the rest of the luncheon, I tried to draw him out, but Steele was through talking. When we parted, he gave me a sober warning.

"You and True should consider your moral responsibility, no matter what you find. Even if it's not actual security, there may be reasons to keep still."

After he left me, I tried to figure it out. If the Air Force was back of this, they must not think much of my intelligence. Or else they had been in such a hurry to get a line on True's investigation that they had no choice but to use Steele. Of course, it was still possible he was doing this on his own,

Either way, his purpose was obvious. He hoped to have us swallow the Soviet-missile answer. If we did, then we would have to keep still, even though we found absolute proof. Obviously, it would be dangerous to print that story.

Thinking back, I recalled Steele's apparent attempt to dismiss the Mantell case. I was convinced now. The Godman Field affair must hold an important clue that I had overlooked. It might even be the key to the whole flying saucer riddle.

CHAPTER VI

SHORTLY after my talk with Steele, I flew to the Coast. For three weeks I investigated sightings that had been reported by airline and private pilots and other competent witnesses.

At first, the airline pilots were reluctant to talk. Most of them remembered the ridicule that had followed published accounts by other airline men. One pilot told me he had been ordered to keep still about his experience - whether by the company or the Air Force, he would not say. But most of them finally agreed to talk, if I kept their names out of print.

One airline captain - I'll call him Blake - had encountered a saucer at night. He and his copilot had sighted the object, gleaming, in the moonlight, half a mile to their left.

"We were at about twelve thousand feet," he said, when we saw this thing pacing us. It didn't have any running lights, but we could see the moonlight reflecting from something like bright metal. There was a glow along the side, like some kind of light, or exhaust."

"Could you make out the shape?" I asked.

Blake grinned crookedly. "You think we didn't try? I cut in toward it. It turned in the same direction. I pulled up about three hundred feet, and it did the same. Finally, I opened my throttles and cut in fast, intending to pull tip if we got too close. I needn't have worried. The thing let out a burst of reddish flame and streaked up out of sight. It was gone in a few seconds."

"Then it must have been piloted," I said.

"If not, it had some kind of radar-responder unit to make it veer off when anything got near it. It matched every move I made, until the last one."

I asked him what he thought the saucer was. Blake hesitated, then he gave me a slow grin.

"Well, my copilot thinks it was a space ship. He says no pilot here on earth could take that many G's, when the thing zoomed."

I'd heard some "men from Mars" opinions about the saucers, but this was an experienced pilot.

"You don't believe that?" I said.

"No," Blake said. "I figure it was some new type of guided missile. If it took as many G's as Chuck, my copilot, thinks, then it must have been on a beam and remote-controlled."

Later, I found two other pilots who had the same idea as Chuck. One captain was afraid the flying saucers were Russian; his copilot thought they were Air Force or Navy. I met one airline official who was indignant about testing such missiles near the airways.

"Even if they do have some device to make them veer off," he said, "I think it's a risk. There'll be hell to pay if one ever hits an airliner."

"They've been flying around for two years," a line pilot pointed out. "Nobody's had a close call yet. I don't think there's much danger."

When I left the Coast, I flew to New York. Ken Purdy called in John DuBarry, True's aviation editor, to hear the details. Purdy called him "John the Skeptic." After I told them what I had learned Purdy nodded.

"What do you think the saucers are?" asked DuBarry.

"They must be guided missiles," I said, "but it leaves some queer gaps in the picture."

I had made up a list of possible answers, and I read it to them:

"One, the saucers don't exist. They're caused by mistakes, hysteria, and so on. Two, they're Russian guided missiles. Three, they're American guided missiles. Four, the whole thing is a hoax, a psychological-warfare trick."

"You mean a trick of ours?" said Purdy.

"Sure, to make the Soviets think we could reach them with a guided missile. But I don't think that's the answer - I just listed it as a possibility."

DuBarry considered this thoughtfully.

"In the first place, you'd have to bring thousands of

people into the scheme, so the disks would be reported often enough to get publicity. You'd have to have some kind of device, maybe something launched from highflying bombers, to give the rumors substance. They'd certainly do a better job than this, to put it over. And it wouldn't explain the world-wide sightings. Also, Captain Mantell wouldn't kill himself just to carry out an official hoax."

"John's right," said Purdy. "Anyway, it's too ponderous. It would leak like a sieve, and the dumbest Soviet agent would see through it."

He looked back at my list. "Cross off Number One, There's too much competent testimony, beside the obvious fact that something's being covered up."

"That leaves Russian or American missiles," I said, "as Steele first suggested. But there are some points that just won't fit the missile theory."

"You've left out one answer," said Purdy.

"What's that?"

"Interplanetary."

"You're kidding!" I said.

"I didn't say I believed it," said Purdy. "I just say it's possible."

DuBarry was watching me. "I know how you feel. That's how it hit me when Ken first said it,"

" I've heard it before , " I said. " But I never took

it seriously."

"Maybe this will interest you," Purdy said. He gave me a note from Sam Boal:

"Just talked with D -," the note ran. (D - is a prominent aeronautical engineer, the designer of a world-famous plane.) "He believes the disks may be interplanetary and that the Air Force knows it - or at least suspects it. I'm enclosing sketches showing how he thinks the disks operate."

"He's not the first one who told us that," said Purdy. "We've heard the same thing from other engineers. Over a dozen airline pilots think they're coming from out in space. And there's a rocket expert at Wright Field who's warned Project 'Saucer' that the things are interplanetary. That's why I'm not writing it off."

"Have you read the Project 'Saucer' ideas on space travel?" DuBarry asked me. I told him my copy hadn't reached me. He read me some marked paragraphs in his copy of the preliminary report:

"'There has been speculation that the aerial phenomena might actually be some form of penetration from another planet . . . the existence of intelligent life on Mars is not impossible but is completely unproven . . . the possibility of intelligent life on the Planet Venus is not considered completely unreasonable by astronomers . . . Scientists concede that living organisms might develop in chemical environments which are strange to us . . . in the next fifty years we will almost certainly start exploring space . . . the chance of space travelers existing at planets attached to neighboring stars is very much greater than the chance of space-traveling Martians. The one can be viewed as almost a certainty . . .'"

DuBarry handed me the report. "Here - I practically know it by heart. Take it with you. You can send it back later."

"I know the space-travel idea sounds silly at first," said Purdy, "but it's the only answer that explains all the sightings-especially those in the last century."

He asked DuBarry to give me their file of historic reports. While John was getting it, Purdy went on:

"Be careful about this man Steele. After what he said about 'moral responsibility' I'm sure he's planted."

I thought back to Steele's warning. I told Purdy: "If he had the space thing in mind, maybe he's right. It could set off a panic that would make that Orson Welles thing look like a picnic."

"Certainly it could," Purdy said. "We'd have to handle it carefully-if it turned out to be the truth. But I think the Air Force is making a mistake, if that's what they're hiding. It could break the wrong way and be serious."

John DuBarry came back with the file of old reports.

"It might interest you to know," he said, "that the Air Force checked all these old sightings too."

The idea was still a difficult one for me to believe.

"Those space-travel suggestions might be a trick," I said. "The Air Force may be hinting at that to hide the guided-missile secret."

"Yes, but later on they deny the space thing," said Purdy. "It looks as if they're trying to put people on guard and then play it down, so they won't get scared."

As I put the historic reports file in my brief case, Purdy handed me a letter from an investigator named Hilton, who had been working in the Southwest. I skimmed over his letter.

Hilton had heard of some unusual night sightings in New Mexico. The story had been hushed up, but he had learned some details from a pilot at Albuquerque.

One of these mysterious "flying lights" had been seen at Las Vegas, on December 8, 1948 - just one month before Mantell was killed in Kentucky. It was too dark to make out the shape behind the light, but all witnesses had agreed on its performance. The thing had climbed at tremendous speed, its upward motion shown by a bright green light. Though the green glow was much brighter than a plane's running light, all plane schedules were carefully checked.

"I think they were trying to pin it on a jet fighter," the Albuquerque pilot told Hilton. "But there weren't any jets near there. Anyway, the thing climbed too fast. It must have been making close to nine hundred miles an hour."

The Air Force had also checked balloon release times - apparently just for the record, since no balloon could even approach the saucer's terrific ascent. Again, they drew a blank.

"From the way this was hushed up," Hilton commented, "they seem to be worried about this group of sightings. I've heard two reports that the F.B.I. is tied into the deal somehow, but that's as far as I can get."

"See if you can get any lead on that," Purdy told me. "That F.B.I. business puzzles me. Where would they come in?"

I said I would try to find out. But it was almost four months before we learned the answer: The F.B.I. men had been witnesses. (This was later admitted in an obscure cross-reference in the final Project "Saucer" report. But all official answers to the strange green-light sightings had been carefully omitted. The cases concerned were 223, 224, 225, 226, 227, 230, and 231, which will be discussed later.)

"When you go back to Washington," said Purdy, "see what reaction you get to the interplanetary idea."

I had a pretty good idea what the reaction would be, but I nodded. "O.K. I'll go flag a space ship and be on my way."

"O.K. - gag it up," said Purdy. "But don't sell it short, If by any chance it's true, it'll be the biggest story since the birth of Christ."

CHAPTER VII

IT WAS DARK when the airliner limousine reached La Guardia Field. I had intended taking an earlier plane, but DuBarry persuaded me to stay over for dinner.

We dropped into the Algonquin, next door to True's office building. Halfway through dinner, I asked John what he thought of the space-travel answer.

"Oh, it's possible," he said cautiously. "The time and space angles make it hard to take, but if we're planning to explore space within fifty years, there's no reason some other planet people couldn't do it. Of course, if they've been observing us for over a century, as those old sightings seem to indicate, they must be far ahead of us, at least in technical progress."

Later on, he said thoughtfully, "Even though it's possible, I hate to think it's the answer. just imagine the impact on the world. We'd have to reorient our whole lives - and things are complicated enough already."

Standing at the gate, waiting for my plane to be called, I thought over that angle. Assuming that space travel was the solution - which I still couldn't believe-what would be the effect on the world?

It was a hard thing to picture. So much depended on the visitors from space. What would their purpose be? Would they be peaceful or hostile? Why had they been observing the earth so intensively in the past few years?

I could think of a hundred questions. What would the space people be like? Would they be similar to men and women on earth, or some fearsome Buck Rogerish creatures who would terrify the average American - including myself?

It was obvious they would be far superior to us in many ways. But their civilization might be entirely different. Evolution might have developed their minds, and possibly their bodies, along lines we couldn't even grasp. Perhaps we couldn't even communicate with them.

What would be the net effect of making contact with beings from a distant planet? Would earthlings be terrified, or, if it seemed a peaceful exploration, would we bc intrigued by the thought of a great adventure? It would depend entirely on the space visitors' motives, and how the world was prepared for such a revelation.

The more I thought about it, the more fantastic thc thing seemed.

And yet it hadn't been too long since airplane flight was considered an idiot's dream. This scene here at La Guardia would have seemed pure fantasy in 1900 - thc huge Constellations and DC-6's; the double-decked Stratocruisers, sweeping in from all over the country; the big ships at Pan-American, taking off for points all over the globe. We'd come a long way in the forty-six years since the Wright brothers' first flight.

But space travel!

The gateman checked my ticket, and I went out to the Washington plane. It was a luxury ship, a fifty-two-passenger, four-engined DC-6, scheduled to be in the capital one hour after take-off. By morning this plane, the Aztec, would be in Mexico City.

The couple going up the gangway ahead of me were in their late sixties. Fifty years ago, what would they have said if someone had predicted this flight? The answer to that was easy; at that time, high-school songbooks featured a well-known piece entitled "Darius Green and His Flying Machine." Darius, it seems, was a simple-minded lad who actually thought he could fly.

Fifty years. That was the time the Air Force had estimated it would take us to start exploring space. Would Americans come to accept space travel as matter-of-factly as the people now boarding this plane? The youngsters would, probably; the older ones, as a rule, would be a little more cautious.

In the oval lounge at the rear of the plane, I took out the file of old sighting reports. Glancing through it, I, saw excerpts from nineteenth-century astronomical and scientific journals and extracts from official gazettes. Most of the early sightings had been in Great Britain and on the Continent, with a few reports scattered around the world. The American reports did not begin until the latter part of the century.

The DC-6 rolled out and took off. For a few minutes I watched the lights of Manhattan and Greater New

York twinkling below. The Empire State Building tower was still above us, as the plane banked over the East River.

We climbed quickly, and the familiar outline of Manhattan took shape like a map pin-pointed with millions of lights.

Any large city seen from the air at night has a certain magic, New York most of all. Looking down, I thought: What would a spaceman think, seeing this brilliantly lighted city, the towering skyscrapers? Would other planets have such cities, or would it be something new and puzzling to a visitor from space?

Turning back to the old reports, I skipped through until I found the American sightings. One of the first was an incident at Bonham, Texas, in the summer of 1873.

It was broad daylight when a strange, fast-moving object appeared in the sky, southwest of the town. For a moment, the people of Bonham stared at the thing, not believing their eves. The only flying device then known was the drifting balloon. But this thing was tremendous, and speeding so fast its outlines were almost a blur.

Terrified farmers dived under their wagons. Towns-people fled indoors. Only a few hardy souls remained in the streets. The mysterious object circled Bonham twice, then raced off to the cast and vanished. Descriptions of the strange machine varied from round or oval to cigar-shaped. (The details of the Bonham sighting were later confirmed for me by Frank Edwards, Mutual network newscaster, who investigated this case.)

Twenty-four hours after the Bonham incident, a device of the same description appeared at Fort Scott, Kansas. Panic-stricken soldiers fled the parade ground as the thing flashed overhead. In a few seconds it disappeared, circling toward the north.

Until now, I had supposed that the term "saucer" was original with Kenneth Arnold. Actually, the first to compare a flying object with a saucer was John Martin, a farmer who lived near Denison, Texas. The Denison Daily News of January 25, 1878, gives the following account:

From Mr. John Martin, a farmer who lives some six miles south of this city, we learn the following strange story: Tuesday morning while out hunting, his attention was directed to a dark object high up in the southern sky. The peculiar shape and velocity with which the object seemed to approach riveted his attention and he strained his eves to discover its character. When first noticed, it appeared to be about the size of an orange, which continued to grow in size. After gazing at it for some time Mr. Martin became blind from long looking and left off viewing it for a time in order to rest his eyes. On resuming his view, the object was almost overhead and had increased considerably in size, and appeared to be going through space at wonderful speed. When directly over him it was about the size of a large saucer and was evidently at great height. Mr. Martin thought it resembled, as well as he could judge, a balloon. It went as rapidly as it had come and was soon lost to sight in the heavenly skies. Mr. Martin is a gentleman of undoubted veracity and this strange occurrence, if it was not a balloon, deserves the attention of our scientists.

In the file, I saw a memo DuBarry had written:

"I would take the very early reports with caution. For instance, the one on August 9, 1762, which describes an odd, spindle-shaped body traveling at high speed toward the sun. I recall that Charles Fort accepted this, along with other early sightings, as evidence of space ships. But this particular thing might have been a meteor - meteors as such were almost unknown then. The later reports are more convincing, and it is also easier to check the sources, especially those from 1870 on."

From 1762 to 1870, the reports were meager. Some described mysterious lights in the sky; a few mentioned round objects seen in daylight. Even though they were not so fully documented as later ones, one point struck me. In those days, there was no telegraph, telephone, or radio to spread news rapidly and start a flood of rumors. A sighting in Scotland could not be the cause of a similar one two days later in the south of France.

Beginning in 870, there was a series of reports that went on to the turn of the century. In the London Times, September 26, 1870, there was a description of a queer object that was seen crossing the moon. It was reported as elliptical, with some kind of tail, and it took almost thirty seconds to complete its passage of the moon. Then in 1871, a large, round body was sighted above Marseilles, France. This was on August 1. It moved slowly across the sky, apparently at great height, and was visible about fifteen minutes.

On March 22, 1880, several brilliantly luminous objects were reported seen at Kattenau, Germany.

Sighted just before sunrise, they were described as rising from the horizon and moving from east to west. The account was published in the British Nature Magazine, Volume 22, page 64.

The next report in the file mentioned briefly a strange round object seen in the skies over Bermuda. The source for this account was the Bermuda Royal Gazette. This was in 1885. That same year, an astronomer and other witnesses reported a gigantic aerial object at Adrianople, Turkey. On November 1, the weird apparition was seen moving across the sky. Observers described it as round and four to five times the size of the moon.

This estimate is similar to the Denison, Texas, comparison with an orange. The object would actually be huge to be seen at any great height. But unless the true height were known, any estimate of size would be guesswork.

On March 19, 1887, two strange objects fell into the sea near a Dutch barkentine. As described by the skipper, Captain C. D. Sweet, one of the objects was dark, the other brightly luminous. The glowing object fell with a loud roaring sound; the shipmaster was positive it was not a meteor.

In New Zealand, a year later, an oval-shaped disk was reported speeding high overhead. This was on May 4, 1888. About two years after this, several large aerial bodies were sighted hovering over the Dutch East Indies. Most accounts described them as roughly triangular, about one hundred feet on the base and two hundred feet on the sides. But some observers thought they might be longer and narrower, with a rounded base; this would make them agree with more recent stories of cone-shaped objects with rounded tops seen in American skies.

On August 26, 1894, a British admiral reported sighting a large disk with a projection like a tail. And a year after this, both England and Scotland buzzed with stories of triangular-shaped objects like those seen in the Dutch East Indies. Although many officials scoffed at the stories, more than one astronomer stuck to his belief that the mysterious things might be coming from outer space. Since planes and dirigibles were then unknown, there was no one on earth who could have been responsible for them.

In 1897, sightings in the United States began to be more frequent. One of the strangest reports describes an incident that began on April 9. Flying at a great height, a huge cigar-shaped device was seen in the Midwest. Short wings projected from the sides of the object, according to reports of astronomers who watched it through telescopes.

For almost a week, the aerial visitor was sighted around the Midwest, as far south as St. Louis and as far west as Colorado. Several times, red, green, and white lights were seen to flash in the sky; some witnesses thought the crew of this strange craft might be trying to signal the earth.

On April 16, the thing, whatever it was, disappeared from the Midwest. But on April 19, the same object - or else a similar one - appeared over West Virginia. Early that morning the town of Sisterville was awakened by blasts of the sawmill whistle. Those who went outside their homes saw a strange sight. From a torpedo-shaped object overhead, dazzling searchlights were pointing downward, sweeping the countryside. The thing appeared to be about two hundred feet long, some thirty feet in diameter, with stubby wings and red and green lights along the sides. For almost ten minutes the aerial visitor circled the town, then it swung eastward and vanished.

The next report was published in the U.S. Weather Bureau's monthly Weather Review. On page 115 in the March 1904 issue, there is an account of an odd sighting at sea. On February 24, 1904, a mysterious light had been seen above the Atlantic by crew members of the U.S.S. Supply. It was moving swiftly, and evidently at high altitude. The report was attested by Lieutenant Frank H. Schofield, U.S.N.

On July 2, 1907, a mysterious explosion occurred, in the heavens near Burlington, Vermont. Some witnesses described a strange, torpedo-shaped device circling above. Shortly after it was seen, a round, luminous object flashed down from the sky, then exploded, (Weather Review, 1907, page 310.)

Another cigar-shaped craft was reported at a low altitude over Bridgewater, Massachusetts, in 1905. Like the one at Sisterville, it carried searchlights, which swept back and forth across the countryside. After a few moments, the visitor rose in a steep climb, and the searchlights blinked out.

There was no report for 1909 in America, though an odd aerial object was sighted near the Galapagos Islands. But in 1910, one January morning, a large silvery cigar-shaped device startled Chattanooga. After about five minutes, the thing sped away, appearing over Huntsville, Alabama, shortly afterward. It made a second appearance over Chattanooga the next day, then headed east and was never seen again.

In Popular Astronomy, January 27, 1012, a Dr. F. B. Harris described an intensely black object that he saw crossing the moon. As nearly as he could tell, it was gigantic in size - though again there was no way to be sure of its distance from him or the moon. With careful understatement, Dr. Harris said, "I think a very interesting and curious phenomenon happened that night."

A strange shadow was noted on the clouds at Fort Worth, Texas, on April 8, 19, 3. It appeared to be caused by some large body hovering motionless above the clouds. As the cloud layer moved, the shadow remained in the same position. Then it changed size, diminishing, and quickly disappeared, as if it had risen vertically. A report on this was given in the Weather Bureau Review of that year, Number 4-599 By 1919, dirigibles were of course well known to most of the world. When a dirigible-shaped object appeared over Huntington, West Virginia, in July of that year, there was no great alarm. It was believed to be an American blimp, though the darkness - it was eleven at night - prevented observers from being sure. But a later check-up proved it was not an American ship, nor was it from any country possessing such craft.

For some time after this, there were few authentic reports. Then in 1934, Nicholas Roerich, head of the American-Roerich expedition into Tibet, had a remarkable experience that bears on the saucer riddle.

On pages 361 and 362 of his book Altai Himalaya,

Roerich describes the incident. The expedition party was in the wilds of Tibet one morning when a porter noticed the peculiar actions of a buzzard overhead. He called Roerich's attention to it; then they all saw something high in the sky, moving at great speed from north to south. Watching it through binoculars, Roerich saw it was oval-shaped, obviously of huge size, and reflecting the sun's rays like brightly polished metal. While he trailed it with his glasses, the object suddenly changed direction, from south to southwest. It was gone in a few moments.

This was the last sighting listed before World War II.

When I had finished, I stared out the plane window, curiously disturbed. Like most people, I had grown up believing the earth was the center of everything - life, intelligence, and religion. Now, for the first time in my life, that belief was shaken.

It was a curious thing. I could accept the idea that we would eventually explore space, land on the moon, and go on to distant planets. I had read of the plans, and I knew our engineers and scientists would somehow find a way. It did not disturb my belief in our superiority.

But faced with this evidence of a superior race in the universe, my mind rebelled. For years, I had been accustomed to thinking in comic-strip terms of any possible spacemen - Buck Rogers stuff, with weird-looking space ships and green-faced Martians.

But now, if these sightings were true, the shoe was on the other foot. We would be faced with a race of beings at least two hundred years ahead of our civilization - perhaps thousands. In their eyes , we might look like primitives.

My conjectures before the take-off had just been idle thinking; I had not really believed this could be the answer. But now the question came back sharply. How would we react to a sudden appearance of space ships, bringing that higher race to the earth? If we were fully prepared, educated to this tremendous adventure, it might come off without trouble. Unprepared, we would be thrown into panic.

The lights of Philadelphia showed up ahead, and a thought struck me. What would Philadelphians of 1776 have thought to see this DC-6 flying across their city at three hundred miles an hour? What would the sentries at Valley Forge have done, a year later, if this lighted airliner had streaked over their heads?

Madness. Stampede. Those were the plain answers.

But there was a difference now. We had had modern miracles, radio, television, supersonic planes, and the promise of still more miracles. We could be educated, or at least partly prepared, to accept space visitors.

In fifty years we had learned to fly. In fifty years more, we would be exploring space. Why should we believe such creative intelligence was limited to the earth? It would be incredible if the earth, out of all the millions of planets, proved the only inhabited spot in the whole universe.

But, instinctively, I still fought against believing that the flying saucers were space ships. Eventually, we would make contact with races on other planets; they undoubtedly would someday visit the earth. But if it could be put off . . . a problem for later generations to handle.

If the disks proved American guided missiles, it would be an easier answer.

Looking through the Project "Saucer" report DuBarry had loaned me, I read the space-travel items, hoping to find some hint that this was a smoke screen. On page 18, in a discussion on Mars, I found this comment:

"Reports of strange objects seen in the skies have been handed down through the generations. However, scientists believe that if Martians were now visiting the earth without establishing contact, it could be assumed that they have just recently succeeded in space travel, and that their civilization would be practically abreast of ours. This because they find it hard to believe that any technically established race would come here, flaunt its ability in mysterious ways over the years, but each time simply go way without ever establishing contact."

There could be several answers to that. The Martians might not be able to live in our atmosphere, except in their sealed space ships. They, or some other planet race, could have observed us periodically to check on our slow progress. Until we began to approach their level of civilization, or in some way caused them concern, they would probably see no reason for trying to make contact. But somehow I found a vague comfort in the argument, full of holes though it was.

Searching further, I found other space-travel comments. On one page, the Air Force admitted it was almost a certainty that space travelers would be operating from planets outside the solar system. But on the following page, I discovered this sentence: "Thus, although visits from outer space are believed to be possible, they are thought to be highly improbable."

What was the answer? Was this just a wandering discussion of possibilities, badly put together, or was it a hint of the truth? It could be the first step in preparing America for a revelation. It could also be a carefully thought-out trick.

This whole report might be designed to conceal a secret weapon. If the Air Force or the Navy did have a secret missile, what better way to distract attention? The old sighting reports could have been seized on as a buildup for space travel hints.

Then suddenly it hit me.

Even if it were a smoke screen, what of those old reports?

They still remained to be answered. There was only one possible explanation, unless you discarded the sightings as lies. That meant discrediting many reliable witnesses - naval officers, merchant shipmasters, explorers, astronomers, ministers, and responsible public officials. Besides all these, there had been thousands of other witnesses, where large groups had seen the objects.

The answer seemed inevitable, but I held it off. I didn't want to believe it, with all the changes it might bring, the unpredictable effect upon our civilization.

If I kept on checking I might find evidence that would

bring a different explanation for the present saucers.

DuBarry had put another group of reports in the envelope; this series covered the World War II phase and on up to the outbreak of the saucer scare in the United States. Some of it, about the foo fighters, I already knew. This was tied in with the mystery rockets reported over Sweden. The first Swedish sightings had occurred during the early part of the war. Most of the so-called "ghost rockets" were seen at night, moving at tremendous speed. Since they came from the direction of Germany, most Swedes believed that guided rockets were the answer.

During the summer of 1946, after the Russians had taken over Peenemunde, the Nazi missile test base, ghost rockets again were reported flying over Sweden. Some were said to double back and fly into Soviet areas. Practically all were seen at night, and therefore none had been described as a flying disk. Instead, they were said to be colored lights, red, green, blue, and orange, often blurred from their high speed.

But there was a puzzling complication. Mystery lights, and sometimes flying disks, were simultaneously reported over Greece, Portugal, Turkey, Spain, and even French Morocco. Either there were two answers, or some nation had developed missiles with an incredibly long range.

By January 1947, ghost-rocket sightings in Europe had diminished to less than one a month. Oddly enough, the first disk report admitted by Project "Saucer" was in this same month. The first '47 case detailed by Project "Saucer" occurred at Richmond, Virginia. It was about the middle of April. A Richmond weather observer had released a balloon and was tracking it with a theodolite when a strange object crossed his field of vision. He swung the theodolite and managed to track the thing, despite its high speed. (The actual speed and altitude - the latter determined by a comparison of the balloon's height at various times - have never been released. Nor has the Air Force released this observer's report on the object's size, which Project "Saucer" admitted was more accurate than most witnesses' estimates.)

About the seventeenth of May 1947, a huge oval-shaped saucer ten times longer than its diameter was sighted by Byron Savage, an Oklahoma City pilot. Two days later, another fast-flying saucer was reported at Manitou Springs, Colorado. In the short time it was observed, it was seen to change direction twice, maneuvering at an unbelievable speed.

Then on June 24 came Kenneth Arnold's famous report, which set off the saucer scare. The rest of the story I now knew almost by heart.

When the DC-6 landed at Washington, I had made one decision. Since it was impossible to check up on most of the old sightings, I would concentrate on certain recent reports - cases in which the objects had been described as space ships.

As I waited for a taxi, I looked up at the sky. It was a clear summer night, without a single cloud. Beyond the low hill to the west I could see the stars.

I can still remember thinking, If it's true, then the stars will never again seem the same.

CHAPTER VIII

NEXT MORNING, in the broad light of day, the idea of space visitors somehow had lost its menace. If the disks were space ships, at least they had shown no sign of hostility, so far as I knew. Of course, there was Mantell; but if he had been downed by some weapon on the disk, it could have been self-defense. In most cases, the saucers retreated at the first sign of pursuit.

My mind was still reluctant to accept the space-travel answer, in spite of the old reports. But I kept thinking of the famous aircraft designer who thought the disks were space craft; the airline pilots Purdy had mentioned; Blake's copilot, Chuck. . . .

Now that I recalled it, Blake had been more embarrassed than seemed called for when he told about Chuck. Perhaps he had been the one who believed the saucers were space ships, instead of his absent copilot.

After breakfast, I went over the list of sightings since June 1947. There were several saucers that actually had been described as projectile-like ships. The most famous of all was the Eastern Airlines case.

It was 8:30 P.M., July 23, 1948, when an Eastern Airlines DC-3 took off from Houston, Texas, on a flight to Atlanta and Boston. The airliner captain was

Clarence S. Chiles. During the war, he had been in the Air Transport Command, with the rank of lieutenant colonel. He had 8,500 flying hours. His first officer was John B. Whitted, a wartime pilot on B-29's. Both men were known in Eastern as careful, conservative pilots.

It was a bright, moonlit night, with scattered clouds overhead. The DC-3 was twenty miles west of Montgomery, at 2:45 A.M., when a brilliant projectile-like craft came hurtling along the airway.

Chiles saw it first and took it to be a jet plane. But the next instant both pilots saw that this was no jet fighter.

"It was heading southwest," Chiles said later, "exactly opposite to our course. Whatever it was, it flashed down toward us at terrific speed. We veered to the left. It veered sharply, too, and passed us about seven hundred feet to the right. I saw then that it had no wings."

The mystery ship passed on Whitted's side, and he had a fairly close look.

"The thing was about one hundred feet long, cigar-shaped, and wingless," he described it. "It was about twice the diameter of a B-twenty-nine, with no protruding fins."

Captain Chiles said the cabin appeared like a pilot compartment, except for its eerie brilliance. Both he and Whitted agreed it was as bright as a magnesium flare. They saw no occupants, but at their speed this was not. surprising.

"An intense dark-blue glow came from the side of the ship," Chiles reported. (It was later suggested by engineers that the strange glare could have come from a power plant of unusual type.) "It ran the entire length of the fuselage - like a blue fluorescent light. The exhaust was a red-orange flame, with a lighter color predominant around the outer edges."

Both pilots said the flame extended thirty to fifty feet behind the ship. As it passed, Chiles noted a snout like a radar pole. Both he and Whitted glimpsed two rows of windows.

"Just as it went by," said Chiles, "the pilot pulled up as if he had seen the DC-three and wanted to avoid its. There was a tremendous burst of flame from the rear. It zoomed into the clouds, its jet wash rocking our DC-three."

Chiles's estimate of the mystery ship's speed was between five hundred and seven hundred miles an hour.

As the object vanished, Chiles went back into the cabin to check with the passengers. Most had been asleep or were drowsing. But one man confirmed that they were in their right senses. This passenger, Clarence McKelvie of Columbus, Ohio, told them (and a Project "Saucer" team later) that he had seen a brilliant streak of light flash past his window. It had gone too swiftly for him to catch any details.

The A.P. interviewed Mr. McKelvie soon after he landed, and ran the following story:

" Kennett Square , Pa. , July 24 (AP) . Clarence L.

McKelvie, assistant managing editor of the American Education Press, said he was the only passenger on the EAL Houston-Boston plane who was not asleep when the phantom craft was sighted.

"'I saw no shape or form,' Mr. McKelvie said. 'I was on the right side of the plane, and suddenly I saw this strange eerie streak out of my window. It was very intense, not like lightning or anything I had ever seen.'

"The Columbus man said he was too startled and the object moved too quickly for him to adjust his eyes to it."

In Washington, Air Force officials insisted they could shed no light on the mystery. Out in Santa Monica, General George C. Kenney, then chief of the Strategic Air Command, declared the Air Force had nothing remotely like the ship described.

"I wish we did," General Kenney told reporters. "I'd sure like to see that."

The publicized story of this "space ship" set off another scare - also the usual cracks about screwball pilots. But Chiles and Whitted were not screwballs; they were highly respected pilots. The passenger's confirmation added weight. But even if all three had been considered deluded, the Air Force investigators could not get around the reports from Robbins Air Force Base.

Just about one hour before the DC-3 incident, a strange flaming object came racing southward through the night skies over Robbins Field, at Macon, Georgia. Observers at the air base were astounded to see what appeared to be a huge, wingless craft streak overhead, trailing a varicolored exhaust. (The witnesses' description tallied with those of Chiles and Whitted.) The mystery ship vanished swiftly; all observers agreed that it disappeared from the line of sight just like a normal aircraft.

While I was working on this case, a contact in Washington gave me an interesting tip.

"Within forty-eight hours after that Eastern sighting, Air Force engineers rushed out blueprint plans and elevations of the 'space ship,' based on what the two pilots told them."

Whether or not this was true, I found that the Air Force engineers did compute the probable speed and lift of the mystery craft. The ship was found to be within the bounds of aerodynamic laws for operations in our atmosphere. Here is the Air Force statement:

"Application of the Prandtl theory of lift indicated that a fuselage of the dimensions reported by Chiles and Whitted could support a load comparable to the weight of an aircraft of this size, at flying speeds in the sub-sonic range." (This supports Chiles's estimate of 500-700 m.p.h.)

Four days after the space-ship story was published, a Navy spokesman was quoted as hinting it might have been a high-atmosphere rocket gone astray from the proving grounds in New Mexico. The brief report appeared on the editorial page of the Washington Star on July 28, 1947. It ran as follows:

" The Navy says that naval technicians have been

testing a 3,000-mile-per-hour rocket in New Mexico. If one went astray, it could travel across our continent in a short time."

At first glance I thought this might be the real answer to the Chiles-Whitted case. But after a few minutes I saw it was almost impossible.

First, rockets at White Sands are launched and controlled with utmost care. There have been no reported cases of such a long-distance runaway.

Second, if such a rocket had gone astray, it would certainly have caused wild confusion at White Sands until they found where it landed. Hundreds of people would have known about it; the story would be certain to leak out.

Third, such a rocket would have had to travel from White Sands to Macon, Georgia, then circle around south of this city for over forty minutes. (If it had kept on at the speed observed at Robbins Field, it would have passed Montgomery long before the DC-3 reached the area.) In addition, the rocket would have had to veer sharply away from the airliner, as both pilots testified, and then zoom into the clouds. No high-atmosphere test rocket has automatic controls such as this would require. And if it had gone astray from White Sands, the station's remote control would no longer be guiding it.

The Eastern Airlines "space ship," then, was not just a fugitive rocket. But it could be a new type of aircraft, something revolutionary, developed in absolute secrecy.

Other airline pilots had reported flying disks racing along the airways, though none that I knew of had described projectile-like objects. Chiles and Whitted insisted the mystery ship was not a disk, and the report from Robbins Field agreed on this point. Man-made devices or not, it seemed fairly certain there was more than one type of saucer.

The more I studied the evidence, the harder it was to believe that this was an earth-made ship. Such a wingless rocket ship would require tremendous jet power to keep it in the air. Even our latest jet bombers could not begin to approach its performance.

Going back over the Project "Saucer" preliminary report, I found strong evidence that the Air Force was worried. In their investigation, Project teams had screened 225 military and civilian flight schedules. After nine months, they reported that the mysterious object was no conventional aircraft.

On April 27, 1949, the Air Force admitted that Project "Saucer" had failed to find the answer. The "space ship" was officially listed as unidentified.

"But Wright Field is still working on it," an Air Force officer told me. "Both Chiles and Whitted are responsible pilots, and McKelvie has a reputation for making careful statements. Even without the Robbins Field confirmation, no one could doubt that they saw something."

The Chiles-Whitted "space ship" was not the first of this type to be reported. Another wingless aircraft was sighted in August 1947, by two pilots for an Alabama flying service. It was at Bethel, Alabama, just after sunset, when a huge black wingless craft swept across their course. Silhouetted against the evening sky, it loomed larger than a C-54. The pilots saw no wings, motors, or jet exhausts.

Swinging in behind the mystery ship, they attempted to follow. But at their speed of 170 m.p.h. they were quickly outdistanced. Careful checking showed there were no other planes nearby that could have been mistaken for this strange craft.

On New Year's Day, 1948, a similar rocket-shaped object was sighted at Jackson, Mississippi. It was first seen by a former Air Force pilot and his passenger, and later by witnesses on the ground. Before the pilot could begin to close in, the odd wingless ship pulled away. Speeding up from 200 to 500 m.p.h., it swiftly disappeared.

Besides these two cases, already on record, I had the tips Purdy had given me. One wingless ship was supposed to have been seen three or four days before the Chiles-Whitted sighting; like the thing they reported, the unidentified craft was a double-decked "space ship" but moving at even higher speed. At first I ran into a stone wall trying to check this story. Then I found a lead conforming that this was a foreign report. It finally proved to be from The Hague.

The tip had been right. This double-decked, wingless ship had been sighted on July 20, 1948 - four days before the Eastern case. Witnesses had reported it at a high altitude, moving at fantastic speed.

While working on this report, I verified another tip. We had heard a rumor of a space-ship sighting at Clark

Donald Keyhoe

Field, in the Philippine Islands. Although I didn't learn the date, I found that there was such a record.

(In the final Project "Saucer" report, the attempt to explain away this sighting was painfully evident. Analyzing this case, Number 206, the Air Force said: "If the facts are correct, there is no astronomical explanation. A few points favor the daytime meteor hypothesis - snow-white color, speed faster than a jet, the roar, similarity to sky-writing and the time of day. But the tactics, if really performed, oppose it strenuously: the maneuvers in and out of cloud banks, turns of 180 degrees or more, Possibly these were illusions, caused by seeing the object intermittently through clouds. The impression of a fuselage with windows could even more easily have been a sign of imagination."

(With this conjecture, Project "Saucer" listed the sighting as officially answered. The Hague space-ship case was unexplained.)

In following up the Jackson and Bethel reports, I talked with two officials in the Civil Aeronautics Administration. One of these was Charley Planck, who handled public relations. I found that the pilots concerned had good records; C.A.A. men who knew them discounted the hoax theory.

"Charley, there's a rumor that airline pilots have been ordered not to talk," I told Planck. "You know anything about it?"

"You mean ordered by the Air Force or the companies?" he said.

"The Air Force and the C.A.A."

"If the C.A.A.'s in on it, it's a top-level deal," said Charley. "I think it's more likely the companies - with or without a nudge from the Air Force."

While we were talking, an official from another agency came in. Because the lead he gave me was off the record, I'll call him Steve Barrett. I knew Steve fairly well. We were both pilots with service training; our paths had crossed during the war, and I saw him now and then at airports around Washington.

When the saucer scare first broke, Steve had been disgusted. "Damn fools trying to get publicity," he snorted. "The way Americans fall for a gag! Even the Air Force has got the jitters."

So I was a little surprised to find he now thought the disks were real.

"What sold you?" I asked.

"The radar reports," said Steve. "I know of half a dozen cases where they've tracked the things. One was in Japan. The thing was climbing so fast no one believed the radarmen at first. Then they got some more reports. One was up in Canada. There was a case in New Mexico, and I think a Navy destroyer tracked a saucer up in the North Atlantic."

"What did they find out?" said Charley Planck.

Steve shrugged. "I don't know all the answers. Whatever they are, the things can go like hell."

I had a hunch he was holding back. I waited until he had finished with Charley, and then went, down the hall with him.

"You think the saucers are guided missiles?" I said. "If I thought so, I wouldn't be talking," he said flatly, "That's not a dig at you. But I was cleared last year for some secret electronics work, and it might be used in some way with guided missiles."

"I didn't know that, Steve."

"It's O.K.," he said. "I don't mind talking, because can't believe the saucers are guided missiles. Maybe few of the things sighted out in the Southwest have beer our test rockets, but that doesn't explain the radar reports in Canada and Japan."

"I'd already heard about a radar case in Labrador," I told Steve. He looked at me quickly.

"Where'd you pick that up;"

"True passed it on to me," I said.

"They've had some trouble tracking the things, they maneuver so fast," said Steve. "It sounds crazy, but I've been told they hit more than ten thousand miles an hour."

"You believe it.?"

"Well, it's not impossible. Those saucers were tracked about fifty miles up, where there's not much resistance."

The elevator door opened. Steve waited until we were outside of the Commerce Building.

"There's one other thing that gets me," he said. "Unless the radar boys are way off, some of those saucers are enormous. I just can't see a guided missile five hundred feet in diameter." He stopped for a moment. "I suppose this will sound screwy to you - "

"You think they're interplanetary," I said.

Steve was quickly on the defensive. "I haven't bought it yet, but it's not as crazy as it sounds."

Without mentioning names, I told him about the aircraft designer and the airline pilots.

"They're in good company," said Steve. "You know the Air Institute?"

"Sure - the Air Force school down at Montgomery."

"Six months ago, I was talking with an officer who'd been instructing there." Steve looked at me, deadly serious. "He told me they are now teaching that the saucers are probably space ships."

CHAPTER IX

THREE DAYS after my meeting with Steve Barrett, I was on a Mainliner 300, starting, a new phase of the saucer investigation. By the time I returned, I hoped to know the truth about Project "Saucer."

As the ship droned westward, fourteen thousand feet above the Alleghenies, I thought of what Steve had told me. I believed, that he had told me about the radar tracking. And I was fairly sure he believed the Air Institute story. But I wasn't so certain the story itself was true.

It would hardly be a gag; Steve wasn't easily taken in. It was more likely that one Institute officer, or perhaps several, believed the saucers were space craft and aired their personal opinions. The Institute wasn't likely to give an official answer to something that Project "Saucer" still declared unsolved.

If it were possible to get an inside look at Project "Saucer" operations, I could soon tell whether it was an actual investigation or a deliberate cover-up for something else. Whichever it was, the wall of official. secrecy still hid it.

As a formality, I had called the Pentagon again and asked to talk with some of the Project officers. As I expected, I was turned down. The only alternative was to dig out the story by talking with pilots and others who had been. quizzed by Project teams. I had several leads, and True had arranged some interviews for me.

My first stop was Chicago, where I met an airline official and two commercial pilots. I saw the pilots first. Since they both talked in confidence, I will not use their right names. One, a Midwesterner I already knew, I'll call Pete Farrell; the other, a wartime instructor, Art Green.

Pete was about thirty-one, stocky, blue-eyed, with a pleasant, intelligent face. Art Green was a little older, a lean, sunburned, restless man with an emphatic voice. Pete had served with the Air Force during the war; he was now part owner of a flying school, also a pilot in the Air National Guard. Green was working for an air charter service

We met at the Palmer House. Art Green didn't need much prompting to talk about Project "Saucer." After reporting a disk, seen during a West Coast Right, he had been thoroughly grilled by a Project "Saucer" team.

"They practically took me apart," he said irritably. "They've got a lot of trick questions. Some of 'em are figured out to trip up anybody faking a story. The way they worked on me, you'd think I committed a murder.

"Then they tried to sell me on the idea I'd seen a balloon, or maybe a plane, with the sun shining on it when it banked. I told them to go to the devil - I knew what I saw. After seventeen years, I've got enough sense to tell a ship or a balloon when I see it."

"Did they believe you?" I asked him.

"If they did, they didn't let on. Two of 'em acted as if they thought I was nuts. The other guy-I think he was Air Force Intelligence - acted decent. He said not to get steamed up about the Aero-Medical boys; it was their job to screen out the crackpots.

"And on top of that, I found out later the F.B.I. had checked up on me to find out if I was a liar or a screwball. They went around to my boss, people in my neighborhood - even the pilots in my outfit. My outfit's still razzing me. I wouldn't report another saucer if one flew through my cockpit."

Pete Farrell hadn't encountered any Project "Saucer" teams personally, but he had some interesting angles. Some of the information had come from commercial and private pilots in the Midwest, part of it through National Guard contacts.

"I can tell you one thing," Pete said. "Guard pilots got the same order as the Air Force. If we saw anything peculiar flying around, we were to do our damnedest to identify it."

"What about trying to bring one down? I've heard that was in one order."

Pete hesitated for a second. "Look, I told you that much because it's been in the papers. But I'm still in the Guard. I can't tell you the order itself. It was confidential."

"Well, I'm not in the Guard," said Art Green. He lit a cigarette, blew out the match. "Why don't you look into the Gorman case? Get thc dope on that court-martial angle."

I'd heard of the Gorman case, but the court-martial thing was new to me. Gorman, I recalled, was a fighter pilot in the North Dakota Air National Guard. He had a mystifying encounter with a strange, fast-moving "light" over Fargo Airport in the fall of 1948.

"That case is on my list," I told Green. "But I don't remember anything about a court-martial."

"It wasn't in the papers. But all the pilots up that way know about it. In his report, Gorman said something about trying to ram the thing. The idea got around that Air Force orders had said to try this. Anyway, it got into the papers and Gorman almost got court-martialed. If his family hadn't had some influence in the state, the Air Force probably would have pushed it."

"Are you sure about this?" I said. "You know how those things build up."

"Ask Gorman," he said. "Or ask some of the pilots at Fargo."

Before I left them, Green double-checked my report on his sighting, which Hilton had forwarded. As in the majority of cases, he had seen just one disk. It had hovered at a very high altitude, gleaming in the sun, then had suddenly accelerated and raced off to the north.

"I couldn't tell its size or speed," said Green. "But if it was as high as I think, it must have been pretty big."

Pete told me later that Green believed the disk had been at least twenty miles high, because it was well above clouds at thirty thousand feet.

"It's kind of hard to believe," said Pete. "The thing would have to be a lot bigger than a B-twenty-nine, and the speed over two thousand miles an hour."

"You know what they said about the Mantell saucer," I reminded him. "Some of the Godman Field people said it was at least three hundred feet in diameter."

"I've heard it was twice that," said Pete.

"You know any Kentucky National Guard pilots?" I asked.

"One or two," said Pete. "But they couldn't tell me anything. It was hushed up too fast."

That evening I talked with the airline official, whom I knew well enough to call by his first name. I put it to him bluntly.

"Dick, if you're under orders not to talk, just tell me. Fm trying to find out whether Project 'Saucer' has muzzled airline pilots."

"You mean the ones who've sighted things? Perhaps, in a few cases. But most of the pilots know what happened to Captain Emil Smith, on United, and those Eastern pilots. They keep still so they won't be laughed at. Also the airlines don't like their pilots to talk for publication."

"I've heard of several cases," I said, "where Air Force

Intelligence is supposed to have warned pilots to keep mum. Two of the reports come pretty straight."

He made a gesture. "That could be. I'm not denying that airline pilots - and that includes ours - see these things all the time. They've been sighted on the Seattle-Alaska route, and between Anchorage and Japan. I know of several saucers that pilots have seen between Honolulu and the mainland. Check with Pan-American - you'll find their pilots have seen them, too."

"What happens to those reports?"

"They go to Operations," said Dick. "Of course, if something really important happens, the pilot may radio the tower before he lands. Then the C.A.A. gets word to the Air Force, and they rush some Intelligence officers to quiz the pilots. if it's not too hot, they'd come from Wright Field - regular Project 'Saucer' teams. Otherwise, they'd send the nearest Intelligence officers to take over temporarily."

I asked him if he had ever been in on one of thee sessions. Dick said he hadn't.

"But a couple of pilots talked to me later. They said these Air Force men seemed quite upset about it; they pounced on everything these boys said about the thing's appearance - how it maneuvered and so on."

"What do your pilots think the saucers are?"

Dick gave me a slightly ironic grin. "Why ask me? Captain Blake says you've been getting it firsthand."

"I wasn't pulling a fast one," I protested. "We're not going to quote actual names or sources, unless people. O.K. it."

"Sure, I know that," said Dick. "But you've got the answer already. Some pilots say interplanetary, some say guided missiles. A few - a very few - still think it's all nonsense, because they haven't seen any."

"What do you think?"

"I don't know the answer," said Dick, "but I'm positive of one thing. Either the Air Force is sitting on a big secret, or they're badly scared because they don't know the answer."

During the next week or so, I covered several northwest and mountain states. Although I was chiefly trying to find out about Project "Saucer," I ran onto two sightings that were not on my list.

One of these had occurred in California, at Fairfield Suisan Air Force Base. A Seattle man who had been stationed there gave me the details. It was on the night of December 1918, with unusually high winds sweeping across the airfield. At times the gusts reached almost seventy miles an hour. Suddenly a weird ball of light flashed into view, at a height of a thousand feet. As the men on the base watched it, astonished, the mysterious light abruptly shot skyward. In an incredibly short time, it reached an altitude of twenty thousand feet and vanished.

"Was there any shape outlined behind the light?" I asked the Seattle man.

"Nobody saw any," he replied. "It looked just like I said - a ball of light, going like a streak."

"Did it leave any smoke behind it?"

"You mean like an engine, or a jet?" He shook his head. "Not a thing. And it didn't make a sound - even when it shot up like that."

"Did you hear any guesses about it, or reports later on?"

"Some major who didn't see it said it must have been a balloon. Anybody with brains could see that was screwy. No balloon ever went up that fast - and besides, the thing was going against the wind."

The second incident occurred at Salmon Dam, Idaho, on August 13, 1947. When I heard the date, it sounded familiar. I checked my sightings file and saw it was the same day as the strange affair at Twin Falls, Idaho.

In the Twin Falls case, the disk was sighted by observers in a canyon. There was one interesting difference from the usual description. This disk was sky-blue, or else its gleaming surface somehow reflected the sky because of the angle of vision. Although it was not close to the treetops, the observers were amazed to see the trees whip violently when the disk raced overhead, as though the air was boiling from the object's swift passage.

At Salmon Dam, that same day, two miners heard an odd roaring sound and stared into the sky. Several miles away, two brightly gleaming disks were circling at high speed.

"It was like two round mirrors whirling around the sky," one of the men was later quoted as saying. "They couldn't have been any ordinary planes; not round like that. And they were going too fast."

During this part of my trip, I also was told that one saucer had fallen into a mountain lake. This came to me secondhand. The lone witness was said to have rushed over to his car to get his camera as the disk approached. When it plunged toward the lake, he was so startled that he failed to snap the picture until the moment it struck. This story sounded so flimsy that I didn't bother to list it.

Months later, a Washington newsman confirmed at least part of the lake story. When he first related it, I thought he had fallen for a gag.

"I heard that yarn," I said. "Don't tell me you believe it?"

"I come from Idaho," he told me. "And I happen to know the fellow who took the picture. Maybe it wasn't a disk, but something fell into that lake."

"Did you see the picture?"

"Yes, at the Pentagon." At my surprised look, he added, "That was long before they clamped down. I was talking to an Air Force officer about this lake thing, and he showed me the picture."

"What did it look like?"

"You couldn't tell much about it-just a big splash and a

blur where something went under. Maybe a magnifying glass would bring it out, but I didn't get a chance to try it."

It was early in 1950 when he told me this. I asked at the Pentagon if this picture was in the Wright Field files, and if so whether I could see it. My inquiries drew blank looks. No one remembered such a photograph. And even if it were in the Project "Saucer" files, I couldn't see it.

This was more than two months after Project "Saucer" had been officially closed and its secrets presumably all revealed.

The rest of my interviews during this 1949 trip helped to round out my picture of Project "Saucer" operations.

Some witnesses seemed afraid to talk; a few flatly refused. I found no proof of official pressure, but I frequently had the feeling that strong hints had been dropped.

Though one or two witnesses showed resentment at investigators' methods, most of them seemed more annoyed at the loss of time involved. One man had been checked first by the police, then by the sheriff's office; an Air Force team had spent hours questioning him, returning the next day, and finally the F.B.I. had made a character check. What he told me about the Air Force interrogation confirmed one of Art Green's statements.

"One Intelligence captain tried to tell me I'd seen a weather balloon. I called up the airport and had them check on release schedules. They said next day it didn't fit any schedules around this area. Anyway, the wind wasn't right, because the thing I saw was cutting into the wind at a forty-five-degree angle."

Other witnesses told me that investigators had suggested birds, meteors, reflections on clouds, shooting stars, and starshells as probable explanations of what they had seen. I learned of one pilot who had been startled by seeing a group of disks racing past his plane. Air Force investigators later suggested that he had flown through a flock of birds, or perhaps a cluster of balloons,

On the flight back to Washington, I reread all the information the Air Force had released on Project "Saucer." Suddenly a familiar phrase caught my eye. I read over the paragraph again:

"Preliminary study of the more than 240 domestic and thirty foreign incidents by Astro-Physicist Hynek indicates that an over-all total of about 30% can probably be explained away as astronomical phenomena."

Explained away

I went through the report line by line. On page 17 I found this:

"Available preliminary reports now indicate that a great number of sightings can be explained away as ordinary occurrences which have been misrepresented as a result of human errors."

On page 22 I ran onto another use of the phrase:

"The obvious explanation for most of the spherical-shaped objects reported, as already mentioned, is that they are meteorological or similar type balloons. This, however, does not explain reports that they travel at high speed or maneuver rapidly. But 'Saucer' men point out that the movement could be explained away as an optical illusion or actual acceleration of the balloon caused by a gas leak and later exaggerated by observers. There are scores of possible explanations for the scores of different type sightings reported."

Explained away . . . It might not mean anything. It could be just an unfortunate choice of words. But suppose that the real mission of Project "Saucer" was to cover up something. Or that its purpose was to investigate something serious, at the same time covering it up, step by step. The Project "Saucer" teams, then, would check on reports and simultaneously try to divert attention from the truth, suggesting various answers to explain the sightings. Back at Wright Field, analysts and Intelligence officers would go over the general picture and try to work up plausible explanations, which, if necessary, could even be published.

"Explaining away" would be one of the main purposes of Project personnel. These words would probably be used in discussions of ways and means; they would undoubtedly would be used in secret official papers. And since this published preliminary report had been made up from censored secret files, the use of those familiar words might have been overlooked, since, read casually, they would appear harmless. If the report had been thrown together hastily, the use of these telltale words could be easily understood, and so could the report's strange contradictions.

As an experiment, I fixed the idea firmly in mind that Project "Saucer" was a cover-up unit. Then I went back once more and read the items quoted above. The effect was almost startling.

It was as though I were reading confidential suggestions for diverting attention and explaining away the sightings; suggestions made by Project members and probably circulated for comment.

"Now, wait a minute," I said to myself. "You may be dreaming up this whole thing."

Trying to get back to a neutral viewpoint, I skimmed through the other details of Project operations, as described in the report.

The order creating Project "Saucer" was signed on December 30, 1947. (The actual code name was not "Saucer," but since for some reason the Air Force still has not published the name, I have followed their usage of "Saucer" in its place.)

On January 22, 1948, two weeks after Captain Mantell's death, the project officially began operations. (Preliminary investigation at Godman Field had been done by local Intelligence officers.) Project "Saucer" was set up under the Air Materiel Command at Wright Field.

Contracts were made with an astrophysicist (Professor Joseph Hynek), also a prominent scientist (still unidentified), and a group of evaluation experts (Rand Corporation). Arrangements were made for services by the Air Weather Service, Andrews Field; the U. S. Weather Bureau; the Electronics Laboratory,

Cambridge Field Station; the A.M.C. Aero-Medical Laboratory; the Army and Navy Departments; the F.B.I.; the Department of Commerce, Civil Aeronautics Administration; and various other government and private agencies. In addition, the services of rocket experts, guided-missile authorities, space-travel planners, and others (in the defense services or assigned to them) were made available as desired. Under the heading "How Incidents Are Investigated," the Project "Saucer" report says:

But the hoaxes and crank letters in reality play a small part in Project "Saucer."

Actually, it is a serious, scientific business of constant investigation, analysis and evaluation which thus far has yielded evidence pointing to the conclusion that much of the saucer scare is no scare at all, but can be attributed to astronomical phenomena, to conventional aerial objects, to hallucinations and to mass psychology.

But the mere existence of some yet unidentified flying objects necessitates a constant vigilance on the part of Project "Saucer" personnel and the civilian population. Investigation is greatly stepped up when observers report incidents as soon as possible to the nearest military installation or to Headquarters, A.M.C., direct. A standard questionnaire is filled out under the guidance of interrogators. In each case, time, location, size and shape of object, approximate altitude, speed, maneuvers, color, length of time in sight, sound, etc., are carefully noted. This information is sent in its entirety, together with any fragments, soil photographs, drawings, etc., to Headquarters, A.M.C. Here, highly trained evaluation teams take over. The information is broken down and filed on summary sheets, plotted on maps and graphs and integrated with the rest of the material, giving an easily comprehended over-all picture.

Duplicate copies on each incident arc sent to other investigating agencies, including technical labs within the Air Materiel Command. These are studied in relation to many factors such as guided missile research activity, weather, and many others, atmospheric sounding balloon launchings, commercial and military aircraft flights, flights of migratory birds and a myriad of other considerations which might furnish explanations.

Generally, the flying objects are divided into four groups: Flying disks, torpedo or cigar-shaped bodies with no wings or fins visible in flight, spherical or balloon-shaped objects and balls of light. The first three groups are capable of flight by aerodynamic or aerostatic means and can be propelled and controlled by methods known to aeronautical engineers. As for the lights, their actions - unless they were suspended from a higher object or were the product of halluci-nation - remain unexplained. Eventually, reports are sent back to Project "Saucer" headquarters, often marking incidents closed. The project, however, is a young one-much of its investigation is still under way.

Currently, a psychological analysis is being made by A.M.C.'s Aero-Medical laboratory to determine what percentage of incidents are probably based on errors of the human mind and senses. Available preliminary reports now indicate that a great number can be explained away as ordinary occurrences which have been misrepresented as a result of these human errors.

Near the end of the last page, a paragraph summed tip the report.

"The 'Saucers' are not a joke. Neither are they cause for alarm to the population. Many of the incidents already have answers. Meteors. Balloons. Falling stars. Birds in flight. Testing devices, etc. Some of them still end in question marks."

From what I had learned on this trip, I strongly doubted the answer suggested. All but the "testing devices." What did they mean by that? It could be a hint at guided missiles; they had already mentioned guided-missile research activity in another spot.

But if that was what lay behind this elaborate project, they would hardly be hinting at it. If the answer was space travel, then such hints made sense, They would be part of the cover-up plan. Everyone - including the Soviet Union - knew we were working on guided missiles. It would do no harm to use this as one of the "myriad explanations" for the flying saucers.

I was still trying to figure it out when my plane let down for the landing at Washington. I had hoped by this time to know the truth about Project "Saucer." Instead, it was a deeper mystery than ever.

True, I had found out how they operated - outside of Wright Field. Some of the incidents had been enlightening. By now, I was certain that Project "Saucer" was trying hard to explain away the sightings and hide the real answer.

CHAPTER X

WHEN I reached home, I found a brief letter from Ken Purdy.

Dear Don:

The Mantell and Eastern cases both look good. I don't see how they can brush them off. It looks more like the interplanetary answer to me, but we won't decide on treatment until we're sure. [I had suggested two or three angles, if this proved the real answer.] Who would be the best authority to check our disk operation theory and give us more details on directional control? I'd like to have it checked by two more engineers.

KEN

Next day, I dug out my copy of Boal's interview with D - , the famous aircraft designer.

"Certainly the flying saucers are possible," the designer had told Boal. "Give me enough money and I'll build you one. It might have to be a model because the fuel would be a problem. If the saucers that have been seen came from other worlds, which isn't at all Buck Rogerish, they may be powered with atomic energy or by the energy that produces cosmic rays - which is many times more powerful - or by some other fuel or natural force that our research hasn't yet discovered. But the circular airfoil is quite feasible.

"It wouldn't have the stability of the conventional airplane, but it would have enormous maneuverability - it could rise vertically, hover, descend vertically, and fly at extremely high speed, with the proper power. Don't take my word for it. Check with other engineers."

Before looking up a private engineer I had in mind, I went to the National Advisory Committee for Aeronautics. The N.A.C.A. { the predecessor of NASA - jbh} is America's most authoritative source of aerodynamic knowledge. I knew they had already tried out disk-shaped airfoils, and I asked about this first. I found that two official N.A.C.A. reports, Technical Note 539 and Report 431, discuss tests on circular and elliptical Clark Y airfoils. Both reports state that these designs were found practical.

Later, I talked with one of the top engineers in the N.A.C.A. Without showing him D - 's sketch, I asked how a disk might operate.

"It could be built with variable-direction jet or rocket nozzles," be said. "The nozzles would be placed around the rim, and by changing their direction the disk could be made to rise and descend vertically. It could hover, fly straight ahead, and make sharp turns.

"Its direction and velocity would be governed by the number of nozzles operating, the power applied, and the angle at which they were tilted. They could be pointed toward the ground, rearward, in a lateral direction, or in various combinations.

"A disk flying level, straight ahead, could be turned swiftly to right or left by shifting the angles of the nozzles or cutting off power from part of the group. This method of control would operate in the earth's atmosphere and also, using rocket power, in free space, where conventional controls would be useless."

The method he had described was not the one which D - had outlined.

"What about a rotating disk?" I asked the N.A.C.A. man. "Suppose you had one with a stationary center, and a large circular section rotating around it? The rotating part would have a camber built into it, or it would have slotted vanes."

He gave me a curious look, "Where'd you get that idea about the camber?"

I told him it had come to me from True.

"It could be done," he said. "The slotted-vanes method has already been tried. There's an engineer in Glendale, California, who's built a model. His name's E. W. Kay."

He gave me a few details on how a cambered or slotted-vane rotating disk might operate, then interrupted himself to ask me what I thought the saucers were.

"They're either interplanetary or some secret development," I said. 'What do you think?"

"The N.A.C.A. has no proof they even exist," he answered.

When I left the building a few minutes later, I was still weighing that statement. If the Air Force or the Navy had a secret disk device, the N.A.C.A. would almost certainly know about it. The chances were that any disk-shaped missile or new type of circular aircraft would first have been tested in the N.A.C.A. wind tunnels at Langley Field. If the saucers were interplanetary, the N.A.C.A. - at least top officials - would probably have been in on any discussion of the disks' performance. Either way, the N.A.C.A.'s official attitude could be expected to match the Pentagon's.

After lunch, I took a taxi to the office of the private engineer. Like D - , he has asked that he not be quoted by name. The name I am using, Paul Redell, will serve that purpose. Redell is a well-known aeronautical engineer. He has worked with major aircraft companies and served as a special consultant to government agencies and the industries. He is also a competent pilot.

Although I had known him several years, he refused at first to talk about the saucers. Then I realized he thought I meant to quote him. I showed him some of the material I had roughed out, in which names were omitted or changed as requested.

"All right," Redell said finally. "What do you want to know?"

"Anything you can tell us. But first, your ideas on these sketches." I showed him D - 's drawings and then gave him the high points of the investigation. When I mentioned the mystery-light incident at Fairfield Suisan Air Force Base, Redell sat up quickly.

"The Gorman case again!"

"We heard about some other 'light' cases," I said. "One was at Las Vegas."

"I know about that one. That is, it you mean the green light - wait a minute!" Redell frowned into space for a few seconds, "You say that Fairfield Suisan sighting was on December third? Then the Las Vegas sighting was only a few days later. It was the first week of the month, I'm positive."

"Those light reports have got me stumped," I said. "A light just can't fly around by itself. And those two-foot disks - "

"You haven't worked on the Gorman case?" asked Redell.

I told him I hadn't thought it was coming up on my schedule.

"Leave these sketches here," he said. "Look into that Gorman sighting. Then check on our plans for space exploration. I'll give you some sources. When you get through, come on back and we'll talk it over."

The Gorman "saucer dogfight" had been described in newspapers; the pilot had reported chasing a swiftly maneuvering white light, which had finally escaped him. Judging from the Project "Saucer" preliminary report, this case had baffled all the Air Force investigators. When I met George Gorman, I found him to be intelligent, coolheaded, and very firmly convinced of every detail in his story. I had learned something about his background. He had had college training. During the war, he had been an Air Force instructor, training French student pilots. In Fargo, his home, he had a good reputation, not only for veracity but as a businessman. Only twenty-six, he was part owner of a construction company, and also the Fargo representative for a hardware-store chain. Even knowing all this, I found it hard at first to believe some of the dogfight details. But the ground observers confirmed them.

It was about nine o'clock in the evening, October 1, 1948. Gorman, now an Air National Guard lieutenant, had been on a practice flight in an F-51 fighter. The other pilots on this practice patrol had already landed. Gorman had just been cleared by the C.A.A. operator in the Fargo Airport tower when he saw a fast-moving light below his circling fighter.

From his altitude, 4,500 feet, it appeared to be the tail light of a swiftly flying plane. As nearly as he could tell, it was 1,000 feet high, moving at about 250 m.p.h.

Gorman called the tower to recheck his clearance. He was told the only other plane in the area was a Piper Cub. Gorman Could see the Cub plainly outlined below him. There was a night football game going on, and the field was brightly lighted.

But the Cub was nowhere near the strange light.

As the mystery light raced above the football field. Gorman noticed an odd phenomenon. Instead of seeing the silhouette of a plane, he saw no shape at all around the light. By contrast, he could see the Cub's outline clearly.

Meantime, the airport traffic controller, L. D. Jensen, had also spotted the queer light. Concerned with the danger of collision - he said later that he, too, thought it a plane's tail light - he trained his binoculars on it. Like Gorman, he was unable to distinguish a shape near the light. Neither could another C.A.A. man who was with him in the tower, a Fargo resident named Manuel E. Johnson.

Up in the F-51, Gorman dived on the light, which was steadily blinking on and off.

"As I closed in," he told Project "Saucer" men later, "it suddenly became steady and pulled up into a sharp left turn. It was a clear white and completely roundabout six to eight inches in diameter.

"I thought it was making a pass at the tower. I dived after it and brought my manifold pressure up to sixty, but I couldn't catch the thing."

Gorman reported his speed at full power as 350 to 400 miles per hour. During the maneuvers that followed, both the C.A.A. men watched from the tower. Jensen was using powerful night glasses, but still no shape was visible near the mysterious light. The fantastic dogfight continued for twenty minutes. Gorman described it in detail.

"When I attempted to turn with the light, I blacked out temporarily, owing to excessive speed. I am in fairly good physical condition, and I don't believe there are many, if any, pilots who could withstand the turn and speed effected by the light and remain conscious."

During these sharp maneuvers , the light climbed

quickly, then made another left bank.

"I put my fifty-one into a sharp turn and tried to cut it off," said Gorman. "By then we were at about seven thousand feet, Suddenly it made a sharp right turn and we headed straight at each other. Just when we were about to collide I guess I lost my nerve. I went into a dive and the light passed over my canopy at about five hundred feet. Then it made a left circle about one thousand feet above and I gave chase again."

When collision seemed imminent a second time, the object shot straight into the air. Gorman climbed after it at full throttle.

Just about this time, two. other witnesses, a private pilot and his passenger, saw the fast-moving light. The pilot was Dr. A. D. Cannon, an oculist; his passenger was Einar Nelson. Dr. Cannon later told investigators the light was moving at high speed. He thought it might be a Canadian jet fighter from over the border. (A careful check with Canadian air officials ruled out this answer.) After landing at the airport, Dr. Cannon and Mr. Nelson again watched the light, saw it change direction and disappear.

Meanwhile, Gorman was making desperate efforts to catch the thing. He was now determined to ram it, since there seemed nothing solid behind it to cause a dangerous crash. If his fighter was disabled, or if it caught fire, he could bail out.

But despite the F-51's fast climb, the light still outdistanced him. At 14,000 feet, Gorman's plane went into a power stall, He made one last try, climbing up to 17,000 feet. A few moments later, the light turned in a north-northwest direction and quickly disappeared.

Throughout the dogfight, Gorman noticed no deviation on his instruments, according to the Project "Saucer" report. Gorman did not confirm or deny this when I talked with him. But he did agree with the rest of the Project statement. He did not notice any sound, odor, or exhaust trail.

Gorman's remarks about ramming the light reminded me of what Art Green had said. When I asked Gorman about the court-martial rumor, he gave me a searching glance.

"Where did you hear that?"

"Several places," I told him. "At Chicago, in Salt Lake City - in fact, we've been hearing it all over."

"Well, there's nothing to it," Gorman declared. He changed the subject.

Some time afterward, a Fargo pilot told me there had been trouble over the ramming story.

"But it wasn't Gorman's fault. Somebody else released that report to the A. P. The news story didn't actually say there was an Air Force order to ram it, but the idea got around, and we heard that Washington squawked. Gorman had a pretty rough time of it for a while. Some of the newspapers razzed his story. And the Project 'Saucer' teams really worked on him. I guess they were trying to scare him into saying he was mistaken, and it was a balloon."

When I asked Gorman about this, he denied he'd had

rough treatment by the Project teams.

"Sure, they asked about a thousand questions, and I could tell they thought it might be a hoax at first. But that was before they quizzed the others who saw it."

"Anybody suggest it was a balloon?" I said casually.

"At first, they were sure that's what it was," answered Gorman. "You see, there was a weather balloon released here. You know the kind, it has a lighted candle on it. The Project teams said I'd chased after that candle and just imagined the light's maneuvers - confused it with my own movement, because of the dark."

Gorman grinned. "They had it just about wrapped up - until they talked to George Sanderson. He's the weather observer. He was tracking the balloon with a theodolite, and he showed them his records. The time and altitudes didn't fit, and the wind direction was wrong. The balloon was drifting in the opposite direction. Both the tower men backed him up. So that killed the weather-balloon idea."

The next step by Project "Saucer" investigators had been to look for some unidentified aircraft. This failed, too. Obviously, it was only routine; the outline of a conventional plane would certainly have been seen by Gorman and the men in the tower.

An astronomical check by Professor Hynek ruled out stars, fireballs, and comets - a vain hope, to begin with. The only other conventional answer, as the Project report later stated, was hallucination. In view of all the testimony, hallucination had to he ruled out. Finally, the investigators admitted they had no solution.

The first Project "Saucer" report, on April 27, 1949, left the Gorman "mystery light" unidentified.

In the Saturday Evening Post of May 7, 1949, Sidney Shallett analyzed the Gorman case, in the second of his articles on flying saucers. Shallet suggested this solution: that Gorman had chased one of the Navy's giant cosmic-ray research balloons. Each of these huge balloons is lighted, so that night-flying planes will not collide with the gas bag or the instrument case suspended below. Shallett concluded that Gorman was suffering from a combination of vertigo and confusion with the light on the balloon.

As already mentioned, these huge Navy balloons are filled with only a small amount of helium before their release at Minneapolis. They then rise swiftly to very high altitudes, unless a leak develops. In Shallett's words, "These balloons travel high and fast. . . ."

Fargo is about two hundred miles from Minneapolis. Normally, a cosmic-ray research balloon would have reached a very high altitude by the time it had drifted this far. The only possible answer to its low-altitude sighting would be a serious leak.

If a leaking balloon had come down to one thousand feet at Fargo, it would either have remained at that height or kept on descending. The mystery light was observed at this altitude moving at high speed. If a Cub's outline was visible against the lighted football field, the massive shape of even a partly deflated balloon would have stood out like an elephant. Even before release, the partially inflated gas bags are almost a hundred feet tall. The crowd at the football game would certainly have seen such a monstrous shape above the glare of the floodlights, for the plastic balloons gleam brightly in any light rays. The two C.A.A. men, watching with binoculars, could not possibly have missed it.

For the cosmic-balloon answer to be correct, this leaking gas bag would have had to rise swiftly to seventeen thousand feet - after a loss of helium had forced it down to one thousand. As a balloon pilot, I know this is impossible. The Project "Saucer" report said unequivocally: "The object could outturn and outspeed the F-51, and was able to attain a much steeper climb and to maintain a constant rate of climb far in excess of the Air Force fighter."

A leaking balloon? More and more, I became convinced that Secretary Forrestal had persuaded some editors that it was their patriotic duty to conceal the answer, whatever it was.

That thought had begun to worry me, because of my part in this investigation. Perhaps John Steele had been right, and we shouldn't be trying to dig out the answer. But I had already told Purdy, and he had agreed, that if national security was involved, we would drop the thing completely.

By the time I had proved the balloon answer wrong, I was badly puzzled. The idea of a disembodied light was the hardest thing to swallow that I'd come across so far.

And yet there were the other light reports - the strange sighting at Fairfield Suisan Field, the weird green lights at Las Vegas and Albuquerque. And there was the encounter that Lieutenant H. G. Combs had had one night above Andrews Field, near Washington, D. C.

This incident had occurred on November 18, 1948, six weeks after Gorman's experience. Combs, flying with another lieutenant named Jackson, was about to land his T-6, at 9:45 P.M., when a strange object loomed up near him. It looked like a grayish globe, and it gave off an odd, fuzzy light.

Combs chased the weird object for over ten minutes, during which it appeared to evade every move he made. Once, its speed was nearly six hundred miles an hour, as closely as he could estimate. In a final attempt to identify it, Combs zoomed the T-6 up at a steep angle and flashed his landing lights on it. Before he could get a good look, the globe light whirled off to the east and vanished.

Since Combs's story had been in the newspapers, Project "Saucer" evidently had felt in wise to give some explanation. When I read it, in the preliminary report, I was amazed. Here was the concluding sentence:

"The mystery was cleared up when the object was identified positively as a cluster of cosmic-ray research balloons."

Even one of the giant balloons would have been hard to take as the explanation. Combs was almost sure to have collided with it in his head-on passes. But an entire cluster! I tried to picture the T-6 zooming and twisting through the night sky, with several huge balloons in its path. It would be a miracle if Combs got through without hitting one of them, even if each balloon was lighted. But he had seen only one light; so had Lieutenant Jackson. That would mean all the rest of the balloons were unlighted - an unbelievable coincidence.

It was not until months afterward that I found Project "Saucer" had withdrawn this "solution." In its final report, this case, Number 207, was listed in the "Unidentified" group. How the balloon-cluster explanation ever got into the first report is still a mystery.

When I talked with Gorman, I told him I was baffled by the idea of a light maneuvering through the skies with no airfoil to support it.

"I know," he said. "It got me, too, at first."

"You mean you know the answer?" I demanded.

"It's just my personal opinion," said Gorman. "But I'd rather not have it printed. You see, I got some ideas from all the questions those Project teams asked me. If my hunch turns out to be right, I might be talking about an official secret."

I tried to pry some hint out of him, but Gorman just smiled and shook his head.

"I can tell you this much," he said, "because it's been mentioned in print. There was thought behind every move the light made. It wasn't any radar-responder gadget making it veer away from my ship."

"How do you know that?"

"Because it reacted differently at different times. If it had been a mechanical control, it would have turned or climbed the same way each time I got near it. Instead, it was as if some intelligent mind was directing every turn like a game of chess, and always one move ahead of me. Maybe you can figure out the rest."

That was all I could get out of him. It bothered me, because Combs's report indicated the same thing. I had a strong temptation to skip the space-plans research and tell Redell what Gorman had told me. But Redell had an orderly mind, and he didn't like to be pushed.

Reluctantly, I gave up the idea. I had a feeling Redell knew the answer to the mystery lights, and it wasn't easy to put off the solution.

The letter that came from Art Green, while I was working on the space plans, didn't make it easier:

Dear Keyhoe:

Just heard about your Seattle visit. That Fairfield Suisan thing is on the level; several Air Force pilots have told me about it. When you get to Fargo, ask Gorman what they found when they checked his ship with a Geiger counter. If he says it was negative, then he must be under orders. I happen to know better.

Yours,
ART GREEN

CHAPTER XI

MY FIRST STEP, in checking on our space plans, was to look up official announcements. I found that on December 29, 1948, Defense Secretary James Forrestal had released this official statement:

"The Earth Satellite Vehicle Program, which is being carried out independently by each military service, has been assigned to the Committee on Guided Missiles for co-ordination.

"To provide an integrated program, the Committee has recommended that current efforts be limited to studies and component design. Well-defined areas of such research have been allocated to each of the three military departments."

Appropriation bills had already provided funds for space exploration plans. The Air Force research was indicated by General Curtis E. LeMay, who was then Deputy Chief of Air Staff for Research and Development. In outlining plans for an Air Engineering Design Center at Wright Field, General LeMay included these space-exploration requisites:

"Flight and survival equipment for ultra-atmospheric operations, including space vehicles, space bases, and devices for use therein."

The idea of exploring space is, of course, nothing new. For many years, writers of imaginative fiction have described trips to the moon and distant planets. More recently, comic books and strips have gone in heavily for space-travel adventures.

As a natural result of this, the first serious rocket experiments in this country were labeled screwball stunts, about on a par with efforts to break through the sonic barrier. The latter had been "proved" impossible by aeronautical engineers; as for rocket flight, it was too silly for serious consideration. Pendray, Goddard, and other rocket pioneers took some vicious ridicule before America woke up to the possibilities.

Meantime, German scientists had gone far ahead.

Their buzz bomb, a low-altitude semi-guided missile, was just the beginning. Even the devastating V-2, which soared high into the stratosphere before falling on England, was just a step in their tremendous space program. If the Nazis could have hung on a year or two more, the war might have had a grimly different ending.

When the Allies seized Nazi secrets, some of the German plans were revealed. Among them was one for a huge earth satellite. From this base, which would circle the earth some five hundred miles away, enormous mirrors would focus the sun's rays on any desired spot. The result: swift, fiery destruction of any city or base refusing to surrender.

First publication of this scheme brought the usual jeers. Many people, including some reputable scientists, believed it had been just a propaganda plan that even

Goebbels had discarded as hopeless.

Then the Pentagon announced the U.S. Earth Satellite Vehicle Program, along with plans for a moon rocket, The artificial satellite is to be a large rocket-propelled projectile. In its upward flight, it will have to reach a speed of 23,000 miles an hour, to escape the earth's pull of gravity. At a height of about 500 miles, special controls will turn the projectile and cause it to circle the earth. These controls will be either automatic or operated from the ground, by radar. Theoretically, once such a vehicle is beyond gravity's magnetism, it can coast along in the sky forever. Its rocket power will be shut off; the only need for such power would be if the satellite veered off course. A momentary burst from the jets would be sufficient to bring it back to its orbit.

Circling the earth in about two hours, this first satellite is expected to be used as a testing station. Instruments will record and transmit vital information to the earth - the effect of cosmic rays, solar radiation, fuel required for course corrections, and many other items.

A second space base farther out will probably be the next step. It may be manned, or it may be under remote control like the first. Perhaps the first satellite vehicle will be followed by a compartmented operating base, a sort of aerial aircraft carrier, with other rocket ships operating to and fro on the earth shuttle. The moon rocket is expected to add to our information about space, so that finally we will emerge with an interplanetary space craft.

The first attempts may fail. The first satellite may fall back and have to be guided to an ocean landing. Or its controls might not bring it into the planned orbit. In this case, it could coast on out into space and be lost. But sooner or later, effective controls will be found. Then the manned space ships will follow.

Once in free space, there will be no gravitational pull to offset. The space ship and everything in it will be weightless. Shielding is expected to prevent danger from cosmic rays and solar radiation.

The danger from meteorites has been partly discounted in one scientific study. ("Probability that a meteorite will hit or penetrate a body situated in the vicinity of the earth," by G. Grimminger, Journal of Applied Physics, Vol. 19, No. 10, pp. 947-956, October 1948) In this study, it is stated that a meteorite is unlikely to penetrate the thick shell our space vehicles will undoubtedly have. However, this applies only to the earth's atmosphere. Longer studies, using remote-controlled vehicles in space, may take years before it will be safe to launch a manned space ship. Radar or other devices may have to be developed to detect approaching meteorites at a distance and automatically change a space ship's course. The change required would be infinitesimal, using power for only a fraction of a second.

But before we are ready for interplanetary travel, we will have to harness atomic power or some other force not now available, such as cosmic rays. Navigation at such tremendous speeds is another great problem, on which special groups are now at work. A Navy scientific project recently found that strange radio signals are constantly being sent out from a "hot spot" in the Milky Way; other nebulae or "hot" stars may be similarly identified by some peculiarity in their radio emanations. If so, these could be used as check points in long-range space travel.

Escape from the earth's gravity is possible even now, according to Francis H. Clauser, an authority on space travel plans. But the cost would be prohibitive, with our present rocket motors, and practical operations must wait for higher velocity rocket power, atomic or otherwise. ("Flight beyond the Earth's Atmosphere, "S.A.E.Quarterly Transactions, Vol. 2, No, 4, October 1948.)

Already, a two-stage rocket has gone more than 250 miles above the earth. This is the V-2-Wac Corporal combination. The V-2 rocket is used to power the first part of the flight, dropping off when its fuel is exhausted. The Wac Corporal then proceeds on its own fuel, reaching a fantastic speed in the thin air higher up.

Hundreds of technical problems must be licked before the first satellite vehicle can be launched successfully. Records on our V-2 rockets indicate some of the obstacles. On the take-off, their present swift acceleration would undoubtedly kill anyone inside. When re-entering the earth's atmosphere the nose of a V-2 gets red-hot.

Both the acceleration and deceleration must be controlled before the first volunteers will be allowed to hazard their lives in manned rockets. Willi Ley, noted authority on space-travel problems, believes that pilots may have to accept temporary blackout as a necessity on the take-off. (Two of his books, Rockets and Space Travel and Outer Space, give fascinating and well-thought-out pictures of what we may expect in years to come.)

Some authorities believe that our space travel will be confined to our own solar system for a long time, perhaps forever. The trip to the moon, though now a tremendous project, would be relatively simple compared with a journey outside our system. Escape from the moon, for the return trip, would be easier than leaving the earth; because of its smaller mass, to escape the moon's gravitational pull would take a speed of about 5,000 miles an hour, against 23,000 for the earth. Navigation would be much simpler. Our globe would loom up in the heavens, much larger and brighter than the moon appears to us. Radar beams would also be a guide.

The greatest obstacle to reaching far-distant planet is the time required. In the Project "Saucer" study of space travel, Wolf 359 was named as the nearest star likely to have possibly inhabited areas. Wolf 359 is eight light-years from the earth. The limiting speed in space, according to Einstein's law, would be just under the speed of light - 186,000 miles per second. At this speed, Einstein states, matter is converted into energy. It is a ridiculous assumption, but even if atomic power, or some force such as cosmic rays, made an approach to that speed possible, it would still take eight years to reach Wolf 359. The round trip would take sixteen.

There have been a few scientists who dispute Einstein's law, though no one has disproved it. If the speed of light is not an absolute limit for space ships, then travel to remote parts of the universe may someday be possible.

Otherwise, a trip outside our solar system could be a

lifetime expedition. Most space travel would probably be limited to the planets of our sun - the moon, Mars, Venus, Jupiter, and the others.

Although it may be many years before the first manned space ship leaves the earth, we are already at work on the problems the crews would face. I learned some of the details from a Navy flight surgeon with whom I had talked about take-off problems.

"They're a lot further than that" he told me. "Down at Randolph Field, the Aero-Medical research lab has run into some mighty queer things. Ever hear of 'dead distance'?"

"No, that's a new one."

"Well, it sounds crazy, but they've figured out that a space ship would be going faster than anyone could think."

"But you think instantaneously," I objected.

"Oh, no. It takes a fraction of a second, even for the fastest thinker. Let's say the ship was making a hundred miles a second - and that's slow compared with what they expect eventually. Everything would happen faster than your nerve impulses could register it. Your comprehension would always be lagging a split second behind the space ship's operation."

"I don't see why that's so serious," I said.

"Suppose radar or some other device warned you a meteorite was coming toward you head-on. Or maybe some instrument indicated an error in navigation. By the time your mind registered the thought, the situation would have changed."

"Then all the controls would have to be automatic," I said. I told him that I had heard about plans for avoiding meteorites. "Electronic controls would be faster than thought."

"That's probably the answer," he agreed. "Of course, at a hundred miles a second it might not be too serious. But if they ever get up to speeds like a thousand miles a second, that mental lag could make an enormous difference, whether it was a meteorite heading toward you or a matter of navigation."

One of the problems he mentioned was the lack of gravity. I had already learned about this. Once away from the earth's pull, objects in the space ship would have no weight. The slightest push could send crewmen floating around the sealed compartment.

"Suppose you spilled a cup of coffee," said the flight surgeon. "What would happen?"

I said I hadn't thought it out.

"The Randolph Field lab can tell you," he said. "The coffee would stay right there in the air. So would the cup , if you let go of it. But there's a more serious angle - your breath."

"You'd have artificial air," I began.

"Yes, they've already worked that out. But what about the breath you exhale? It contains carbon dioxide, and if you let it stay right there in front of your face you'd be sucking it back into your lungs. After a while, it would asphyxiate you. So the air has to be kept in motion, and besides that the ventilating system has to remove the carbon dioxide."

"What about eating?" I asked. "Swallowing is partly gravity, isn't it?"

He nodded. "Same as drinking, though the throat muscles help force the food down. I don't know the answer to that. In fact, everything about the human body presents a problem. Take the blood circulation. The amount of energy required to pump blood through the veins would be almost negligible. What would that do to your heart?"

"I couldn't even guess," I said.

"Well, that's all the Aero-Medical lab can do - guess at it. They've been trying to work out some way of duplicating the effect of zero gravity, but there's just no answer. If you could build a machine to neutralize gravity, you could get all the answers, except to the 'dead distance' question.

"For instance, there's the matter of whether the human body would even function without gravity. All down through the stages of evolution, man's organs have been used to that downward pull. Take away gravity, and your whole body might stop working. Some of the Aero-Medical men I've talked with don't believe that, but they admit that long trips outside of gravity might have odd effects.

"Then there's the question of orientation. Here on earth, orienting yourself depends on the feeling you get from the pull of gravity, plus your vision. just being blindfolded is enough to disorient some people. Taking away the pull of gravity might be a lot worse. And of course out in space your only reference points would be distant stars and planets. We've been used to locating stars from points on the earth, where we know their position. But how about locating them from out in space, with a ship moving at great speed? Inside the space ship, it would be something like being in a submarine. Probably only the pilot compartment would have glass ports, and those would be covered except in landing - maybe even then. Outside vision might be by television, so you couldn't break a glass port and let out your pressure.

"But to go back to the submarine idea. It would be like a sub, with this big difference: In the submarine you can generally tell which way is down, except maybe in a crash dive when you may lose your equilibrium for a moment. But in the space ship, you could be standing with your feet on one spot, and another crewman might be - relative to you - standing upside down. You might be floating horizontally, the other man vertically. The more you think about it, the crazier it gets. But they've got to solve all those problems before we can tackle space."

To make sure I had the details right, I checked on the Air Force research. I found that the Randolph Field laboratory is working on all these problems, and many more.

Although plans arc not far enough advanced to make it certain, probably animals will be sent up in research rockets to determine the effect of no gravity before any human beings make such flights. The results could be televised back to the earth.

All through my check-up on space exploration plans, one thing struck me: I met no resistance. There was no official reticence about the program; on the contrary, nothing about it seemed secret.

Even though it was peacetime, this was a little curious, because of the potential war value of an earth satellite vehicle. Even if the Nazi scheme for destruction proved just a dream, an orbiting space base could be used for other purposes. In its two-hour swing around the earth, practically all of the globe could be observed-directly, by powerful telescopes, or indirectly, by a combination of radar and television. Long-range missiles could be guided to targets, after being launched from some point on the earth. As the missiles climbed high into the stratosphere, the satellite's radar could pick them up and keep them on course by remote control.

There were other possibilities for both attack and defense. Ordinarily, projects with wartime value are kept under wraps, or at least not widely publicized. Of course, the explanation might be very simple: The completion of the satellite vehicle was so remote that there seemed no need for secrecy. But in that case, why had the program been announced at all?

If the purpose had been propaganda, it looked like a weak gesture. The Soviets would not be greatly worried by a dream weapon forty or fifty years off. Besides that, the Pentagon, as a rule, doesn't go for such propaganda.

There was only one conventional answer that made

any sense. If we had heard that the Soviets were about to announce such a program, as a propaganda trick, it would be smart to beat them to it. But I had no proof of, any such Russian intention.

The date on Secretary Forrestal's co-ordination announcement was December 30, 1948. One day later, the order creating Project "Saucer" had been signed. That didn't prove anything; winding up the year, Forrestal could have signed a hundred orders. I was getting too suspicious.

At any rate, I had now analyzed the Gorman case and checked on our space plans. Tomorrow I would see Redell and find out what he knew.

CHAPTER XII

'WHEN I called Redell's office I found he had flown to Dallas and would not be back for two days. By the time he returned, I had written a draft of the Gorman case, with my answer to the balloon explanation. When I saw him, the next morning, I asked him to look it over.

Redell lighted his pipe and then read the draft, nodding to himself now and then.

"I think that's correct analysis," he said when he finished. "That was a very curious case. You know, Project 'Saucer' even had psychiatrists out there. If Gorman had been the only witness, I think they'd have called it a hallucination. As it was, they took a crack at him and the C.A.A. men in their preliminary report."

Though I recalled that there had been a comment, I didn't remember the wording. Redell looked it up and read it aloud:

"'From a psychological aspect, the Gorman incident raised the question, "Is it possible for an object without appreciable shape or known aeronautical configuration to appear to travel at variable speeds and maneuver intelligently?"'"

"Hallucination might sound like a logical answer," I said, "until you check all the testimony. But there are just too many witnesses who confirm Gorman's report. Also, he seems like a pretty level-headed chap."

Redell filled his pipe again. "But you still can't quite accept it?"

"I'm positive they saw the light - but what the devil was it? How could it fly without some kind of airfoil?"

"Maybe it didn't. You remember Gorman described an odd fuzziness around the edge of the light? It's in this Air Force report. That could have been a reflection from the airfoil."

"Yes, but Gorman would have seen any solid - " I stopped, as Redell made a negative gesture.

"It could be solid and still not show up," he said.

"You mean it was transparent? Sure, that would do it!"

"Let's say the airfoil was a rotating plastic disk, absolutely transparent. The blurred, fuzzy look could have been caused by the whirling disk. Neither Gorman nor the C.A.A. men in the tower could possibly see the disk itself."

"Paul, I think you've hit it," I said. "I can see the rest of it - the thing was under remote control, radio or radar. And from the way it flew rings around Gorman, whoever controlled it must have been able to see the F-51, either with a television 'eye' or by radar,"

"Or by some means we don't understand," said Redell.

He went on carefully, "In all these saucer cases, keep this in mind: We may be dealing with some totally unknown principle - something completely beyond our comprehension."

For a moment, I thought he was hunting at some radical discovery by Soviet - captured Nazi scientists. Then I realized what he meant.

"You think they're interplanetary," I murmured.

"Why not?" Redell looked surprised. "Isn't that your idea? I got that impression."

"Yes, but I didn't think you believed it. When you said to check on our space plans, I thought you had some secret missile in mind."

"No, I had another reason. I wanted you to see all the problems involved in space travel. If you accept the interplanetary answer, you have to accept this, too - whoever is looking us over has licked all those problems years ago. Technically, they'd be hundreds of years ahead of us - maybe thousands. It has a lot to do with what they'd be up to here."

When I mentioned the old sighting reports, I found that Redell already knew about them. He was convinced that the earth had been under observation a long time, probably even before the first recorded sightings.

"I know some of those reports aren't authentic," he admitted. "But if you accept even one report of a flying disk or rocket-shaped object before the twentieth century, then you have to accept the basic idea. In the last forty years, you might blame the reports on planes and dirigibles. But there was no propelled aircraft until 1903. Either all those early sightings were wrong, or some kind of fast aerial machine has been flying periodically over the earth for at least two centuries.

I told him I was pretty well convinced, but that True faced a problem. There was some conflicting evidence, and part of it seemed linked with guided missiles. I felt sure we could prove the space-travel answer, but we had to stay clear of discussing any weapons that were still a secret.

"I can't believe that guided missiles are the answer to the Godman Field saucer and the Chiles-Whitted case, or this business at Fargo. But we're got to be absolutely sure before we print anything."

"Well, let's analyze it," said Redell. "Let's see if all the saucers could be explained as something launched from the earth."

He reached for a pad and a pencil.

"First, let's take your rotating disk. That would be a lot simpler to build than the stationary disk with variable jet nozzles. With a disk rotated at high speed you get a tremendous lift, whether it's slotted or cambered, as long as there's enough air to work on."

"The helicopter principle," I said.

Redell nodded. "The most practical propulsion would be with two or more jets out on the rim, to spin your rotating section. But to get up enough speed for the jets to be efficient, you'd have to whirl the disk mechanically before the take-off. Here's one way. You could have a square hole in the center; then the disk launching device would have a square shaft, rotated by an engine or a motor. As the speed built up, the cambered disk would ride up the shaft and free itself, rising vertically, with the jets taking over the job of whirling the cambered section.

"The lift would be terrific, far more than any normal aircraft. I don't believe any human being could take the G's involved in a maximum power climb; they'd have to use remote control. When it got to the desired altitude, your disk could be flown in any direction by tilting it that way. The forward component from that tremendous lift would result in a very high speed. The disk could also hover, and descend vertically."

"What about maneuvering?" I asked, thinking of Gorman's experience.

"It could turn faster than any pilot could stand," said Redell. "Of course, a pilot's cockpit could be built into a large disk; but there'd have to be some way of holding down the speed, to avoid too many G's in tight maneuvers."

"Most of the disks don't make any noise," I said. "At least, that's the general report. You'd hear ordinary jets for miles."

"Right, and here's another angle. Ram jets take a lot of fuel. Even with some highly efficient new jet, I can't see the long ranges reported. Some of these saucers have been seen all over the world. No matter which hemisphere they were launched from, they'd need an eight-thousand-mile range, at least, to explain all of the sightings. The only apparent answer would be some new kind of power, probably atomic. We certainly didn't have atomic engines for aircraft in 1947, when the first disks were seen here. And we don't have them now, though we're working on it. Even if we had such an engine, it wouldn't be tiny enough to power the small disks."

"Anyway," I said, "we'd hardly be flying them all over everywhere. The cost would be enormous, and there'd always be a danger of somebody getting the secret if a disk landed."

"Plus the risk of injuring people by radiation. just imagine an atomic-powered disk dropping into a city. The whole idea's ridiculous."

"That seems to rule out the guided-missile answer," I began. But Redell shook his head.

"Disk-shaped missiles are quite feasible. I'm talking about range, speed, and performance. Imagine for a moment that we have disk-type missiles using the latest jet or rocket propulsion - either piloted or remote-controlled. The question is, could such disks fit specific sightings like the one at Godman Field and the case at Fargo?"

Redell paused as if some new thought had struck him.

"Wait a minute, here's an even better test. I happen to know about this case personally. Marvin Miles - he's an aviation writer in Los Angeles - was down at White Sands Proving Ground some time ago. He talked with a Navy rocket expert who was in charge of naval guided-missile projects. This Navy man - he's a commander in the regular service - told Miles they'd seen four saucers down in that area."

"You're sure he wasn't kidding Miles?" I said. Then I remembered Purdy's tip about a White Sands case.

"I told you I checked on this myself," Redell said, a little annoyed. "After Miles told me about it, I asked an engineer who'd been down there if it was true. He gave me the same story, figures and all. The first saucer was tracked by White Sands observers with a theodolite. Then they worked out its performance with ballistics formulas."

Redell looked at me grimly.

"The thing was about fifty miles up. And it was making over fifteen thousand miles an hour!"

One of the witnesses, said Redell, was a well-known scientist from the General Mills aeronautical research laboratory in Minneapolis, which was working with the Navy. (A few days later, I verified this fact and the basic details of Redell's account. But it was not until early in January 1950 that I finally identified the officer as Commander Robert B. McLaughlin and got his dramatic story.)

"Here are two more items Miles told me," Redell went on. "This Navy expert said the saucer actually looked elliptical, or egg-shaped. And while it was being tracked it suddenly made a steep climb - so steep no human being could have lived through it."

"One thing is certain," I said. "That fifty-mile altitude knocks out the rotating disk. Up in that thin air it wouldn't have any lift."

"Right," said Redell. "And the variable jet type would require an enormous amount of fuel. Regardless, those G's mean it couldn't have had any pilot born on this earth."

According to Marvin Miles, this White Sands saucer had been over a hundred feet long. (Later, Commander McLaughlin stated that it was 105 feet.) If this were an American device, then it meant that we had already licked many of the problems on which the Earth Satellite Vehicle designers were supposed to be just starting. Their statements, then, would have to be false - part of an elaborate cover-up.

"If we had such an advanced design," said Redell, "and I just don't believe it possible - would we gamble on a remote-control system? No such system is perfect. Suppose it went wrong. At that speed, over fifteen thousand miles an hour, your precious missile or strato ship could be halfway around the globe in about forty-five minutes. That is, if the fuel held out. Before you could regain control, you might lose it in the sea. Or it might come down behind the Iron Curtain. Even if it were I smashed to bits, it would tip off the Soviets. They might claim it was a guided-missile attack. Almost anything could hap pen."

"It could have a time bomb in it," I suggested. "if it got off course or out of control, it would blow itself up."

Redell emphatically shook his head. "I've heard that idea before, but it won't hold up. What if your ship's controls went haywire and the thing blew up over a crowded city? Imagine the panic, even if no actual damage was done. No, sir - nobody in his right mind is going to let a huge ship like that go barging around unpiloted. It would be criminal negligence.

"If the White Sands calculations were correct, then this particular saucer was no earth-made device. Perhaps in coming years, we could produce such a ship, with atomic power to drive it. But not now."

Redell went over several other cases.

"Take the Godman Field saucer. At one time, it was seen at places one hundred and seventy-five miles apart, as you know. Even to have been seen at all from both places, it would. have to have been huge - much larger than two hundred and fifty feet in diameter. The human eye wouldn't resolve an object that size, at such a distance and height."

It was an odd thing; I had, gone over the Mantell case a dozen times. I knew the object was huge. But I had never tried to figure out the object's exact size.

"How big do you think it was?" I asked quickly. This could be the key I had tried to find.

"I haven't worked it out," said Redell. "But I can give you a rough idea. The human eye can't resolve any object that subtends less than three minutes of arc. For instance, a plane with a hundred-foot wing span would only be a speck twenty miles away, if you saw it at all."

"But this thing was seen clearly eighty-seven miles away - or even more, if it wasn't midway between the two cities. Why, it would have to be a thousand feet in diameter."

"Even larger." Redell was silent a moment. "What was the word Mantell used - 'tremendous'?" I tried to visualize the thing, but my mind balked. One thing was certain now. It was utterly impossible that any nation on earth could have built such an enormous airborne machine. just to think of the force required to hold it in the sky was enough to stagger any engineer. We were years away - perhaps centuries - from any such possibility.

As if he had read my thoughts, Redell said soberly, "There's no other possible answer. It was a huge space ship - perhaps the largest ever to come into our atmosphere."

It was clear now why such desperate efforts had been made to explain away the object Mantell had chased.

"What about that Eastern Airlines sighting?" I asked.

"Well, first," said Redell, "it wasn't any remote-control guided missile. I'll say it again; it would be sheer insanity. Suppose that thing had crashed in Macon. At that speed it could have plowed its way for blocks, right through the buildings. It could have killed hundreds of people, burned the heart out of the city.

"If it was a missile, or some hush-hush experimental job, then it was piloted. But they don't test a job like that on any commercial airways. And they don't fool around at five thousand feet where people will see the thing streaking by and call the newspapers.

"To power a hundred-foot wingless ship, especially at those speeds, would take enormous force. Not as much as a V-two rocket, but tremendous power. The fuel load would be terrific. Certainly, the pilot wouldn't be circling around Georgia and Alabama for an hour, buzzing airliners. I'll stake everything that we couldn't duplicate that space ship's performance for less than fifty million dollars. It would take something brand-new in jets."

Redell paused. He looked at me grimly. "And the way I'd have to soup it up, it would be a damned dangerous ship to fly. No pilot would deliberately fly it that low. He'd stay up where he'd have a chance to bail out."

I told him what I had heard about the blueprints the Air Force was said to have rushed.

"Of course they were worried," said Redell. "And probably they still are. But I don't think they need be; so far, there's been nothing menacing about these space ships."

When I got him back to the Gorman case, Redell drew a sketch on his pad, showing me his idea of the disk light. He estimated the transparent rim as not more than five feet in diameter.

"Possibly smaller," he said. "You recall that Gorman said the light was between six and eight inches in diameter. He also said it seemed to have depth - that was in the Air Force report."

"You think all the mechanism was hidden by the light?"

"Only possible answer," said Redell. "But just try to imagine crowding a motor, or jet controls for rim jets, along with remote controls and a television device, in that small space. Plus your fuel supply. I don't know any engineer who would even attempt it. To carry that much gear, it would take a fair-sized plane. You could make a disk large enough, but the mechanism and fuel section would be two or three feet across, at least. So Gorman's light must have been powered and controlled by some unique means. The same principle applies to all the other light reports I've heard. No shape behind them, high speed, and intelligent maneuvers. That thing was guided from some interplanetary ship, hovering at a high altitude," Redell declared. "But I haven't any idea what source of power it used."

Until then, I had forgotten about Art Green's letter. I told Redell what Art had said about the Geiger counter.

"I knew they went over Gorman's fighter with a Geiger counter," Redell commented. "But they said the reaction was negative. If Green is right, it's interesting. It would mean they have built incredibly small atomic engines. But with a race so many years ahead of us, it shouldn't be surprising. Of course, they may also be using some other kind of power our scientists say is impossible."

I was about to ask him what he meant when his secretary came in.

"Mr. Carson is waiting," she told Redell. "He had a four-o'clock appointment."

As I started to leave, Redell looked at his calendar.

"I hate to break this up; it's a fascinating business What about coming in Friday? I'd like to see the rest of those case reports."

"Fine," I said. "I've got a few more questions, too."

Going out, I made a mental note of the Friday date. Then the figure clicked; it was just three months since I'd started on this assignment.

Three months ago. At that time I'd only been half sure that the saucers were real. If anyone had said I'd soon believe they were space ships, I'd have told him he was crazy.

CHAPTER XIII

BEFORE my date with Redell, I went over all the material I had, hoping to find some clue to the space visitors' planet. It was possible, of course, that there was more than one planet involved.

Project "Saucer" had discussed the possibilities in it! report of April 27, 1949. I read over this section again:

Since flying saucers first hit the headlines almost two years ago, there has been wide speculation that the aerial phenomena might actually be some form of penetration from another planet. Actually, astronomers are largely in agreement that only one member of the solar system beside Earth is capable of supporting life. That is Mars. Even Mars, however, appears to be relatively desolate and inhospitable, so that a Martian race would be more occupied with survival than we are on Earth.

On Mars, there exists an excessively slow loss of atmosphere, oxygen and water, against which intelligent beings, if they do exist there, may have protected themselves by scientific control of physical conditions. This might have been done, scientists speculate, by the construction of homes and cities underground where the atmospheric pressure would be greater and thus temperature extremes reduced. The other possibilities exist, of course, that evolution may have developed a being who can withstand the rigors of the Martian climate, or that the race - if it ever did exist - has perished.

In other words, the existence of intelligent life on Mars, where the rare atmosphere is nearly devoid of oxygen and water and where the nights are much colder than our Arctic winters, is not impossible but is completely unproven. The possibility of intelligent life also existing on the planet Venus is not considered completely unreasonable by astronomers. The atmosphere of Venus apparently consists mostly of carbon dioxide with deep clouds of formaldehyde droplets, and there seems to be little or no water. Yet, scientists concede that living organisms might develop in chemical environments which are strange to us. Venus, however, has two handicaps. Her mass and gravity are nearly as large as the Earth (Mars is smaller) and her cloudy atmosphere would discourage astronomy, hence space travel.

The last argument, I thought, did not have too much weight. We were planning to escape the earth's gravity; Martians could do the same, with their planet. As for the cloudy atmosphere, they could have developed some system of radio or radar investigation of the universe. The Navy research units, I knew, were probing the far-off Crab nebula in the Milky Way with special radio devices. This same method, or something far superior, could have been developed on Venus, or other planets surrounded by constant clouds.

After the discussion of solar-system planets, the Project "Saucer" report went on to other star systems:

Outside the solar system other stars - 22 in number - have satellite planets. Our sun has nine. One of these, the Earth, is ideal for existence of intelligent life. On two others there is a possibility of life.

Therefore, astronomers believe reasonable the thesis that there could be at least one ideally habitable planet for each of the 22 other eligible stars.

(After publication of our findings in True, several astronomers said that many planets may be inhabited. One of these was Dr. Carl F. von Weizacker, noted University of Chicago physicist. On January 10, 1950, Dr. von Weizacker stated: "Billions upon billions of stars found in the heavens may each have their own planets revolving about them. It is possible that these planets would have plant and animal life on them similar to the earth's.")

After narrowing the eligible stars down to twenty-two the Project "Saucer" report goes on:

The theory is also employed that man represents the average in advancement and development. Therefore, one-half the other habitable planets would be behind man in development, and the other half ahead. It is also assumed that any visiting race could be expected to be far in advance of man. Thus, the chance of space travelers existing at planets attached to neighboring stars is very much greater than the chance of space-traveling Martians. The one can be viewed as almost a certainty (if you accept the thesis that the number of inhabited planets is equal to those that are suitable for life and that intelligent life is not peculiar to the Earth) ."

The most likely star was Wolf 359 - eight light-years away. I thought for a minute about traveling that vast distance. It was almost appalling, considered in terms of man's life span. Of course, dwellers on other planets might live much longer.

If the speed of light was not an absolute limit, almost any space journey would then be possible. Since there would be no resistance in outer space, it would be simply a matter of using rocket power in the first stages to accelerate to the maximum speed desired. In the latter phase, the rocket's drive would have to be reversed, to decelerate for the landing.

The night before my appointment with Redell, I was checking a case report when the phone rang. It was John Steele.

"Are you still working on the saucers?" he asked. "If you are, I have a suggestion - something that might be a real lead."

"I could use a lead right now," I told him.

"I can't give you the source, but it's one I consider reliable," said Steele. "This man says the disks are British developments."

This was a new one. I hadn't considered the British. Steele talked for over half an hour, expanding the idea.

The saucers, his informant said, were rotating disks with cambered surfaces - originally a Nazi device. Near the end of the war, the British had seized all the models, along with the German technicians and scientists who had worked on the project.

The first British types had been developed secretly in England, according to this account. But the first tests showed a dangerous lack of control; the disks streaked up to high altitudes, hurtling without direction. Some had been seen over the Atlantic, some in Turkey, Spain, and other parts of Europe.

The British then had shifted operations to Australia, where a guided-missile test range had been set up. (This part, I knew, could be true; there was such a range.) After improving their remote-control system, which used both radio and radar, they had built disks up to a hundred feet in diameter. These were launched out over the Pacific, the first ones straight eastward over open sea. British destroyers were stationed at 100-mile and later 500-mile intervals, to track the missiles by radar and correct their courses. At a set time, when their fuel was almost exhausted, the disks came down vertically and landed in the ocean. Since part of the device was sealed, the disks would float; then a special launching ship would hoist them abroad, refuel them, and launch them back toward a remote base in Australia, where they were landed by remote control.

Since then, Steele said, the disks' range and speed had been greatly increased. The first tests of the new disks was in the spring of 1947, his informant had told him. The British had rushed the project, because of Soviet Russia's menacing attitude. Their only defense in England, the British knew, would be some powerful guided missile that could destroy Soviet bases after the first attack.

In order to check the range and speeds accurately, it was necessary to have observers in the Western Hemisphere - the disks were now traversing the

Pacific. The ideal test range, the British decided, was one extending over Canada, where the disks could be tracked and even landed, If the account was right, said Steele, a base had been set up in the desolate Hudson Bay country. Special radar-tracking stations had also been established, to guide the missiles toward Australia and vessels at sea. These stations also helped to bring in missiles from Australia.

Some of the disk missiles were supposed to have been launched from a British island in the South Pacific; others came all the way from Australia. Still others were believed to have been launched by a mother ship stationed between the Galapagos Islands and Pitcairn.

It was these new disks that had been seen in the United States, Alaska, Canada, and Latin America, Steele's informant had told him. At first, the sightings were due to imperfect controls; the disks sometimes failed to keep their altitude, partly because of conflicting radio and radar beams from the countries below. Responding to some of these mixed signals, Steele said, the disks had been known to reverse course, hover or descend over radar and radio stations, or circle around at high speeds until their own control system picked them up again.

For this reason, the British had arranged a simple detonator system, operated either by remote control or automatically under certain conditions. In this way, no disk would crash over land, with the danger of hitting a populated area. If it descended below a certain altitude, the disk would automatically speed up its rotation, then explode at a high altitude. When radar trackers saw that a disk was off course and could not be realigned, the nearest station then sent a special signal to activate the detonator system. This was always done, Steele had been told, when a disk headed toward Siberia; there had previously been a few cases when Australian-launched disks had got away from controllers and appeared over Europe.

I listened to Steele's account with mixed astonishment and suspicion. It sounded like a pipe dream; but if it was, it had been carefully thought out, especially the details that followed.

At first, Steele said, American defense officials had been completely baffled by the disk reports. Then the British, learning about the sightings, had hastily explained to top-level American officials. An agreement had been worked out. We were to have the benefit of their research and testing and working models, in return for helping to conceal the secret. We were also to aid in tracking and controlling the missiles when they passed over this country.

"And I gather we paid in other ways," Steele said. "My source says this played a big part in increasing our aid to Britain, including certain atomic secrets."

That could make sense. Sharing such a secret would be worth all the money and supplies we had poured into England. If America and Great Britain both had a superior long-range missile, it would be the biggest factor I knew for holding off war. But the long ranges involved in Steele's explanation made the thing incredible.

"How are they powered? What fuel do they use?" I asked him.

"That's the one thing I couldn't get," said Steele. "This man told me it was the most carefully guarded secret of all. They've tapped a new source of power."

"If he means atomic engines," I said, "I don't believe it. I don't think anyone is that far along."

"No, no," Steele said earnestly, "he said it wasn't that. And the rest of the story hangs together."

Privately, I thought of two or three holes, but I let that go.

"If it's British," I said, "do you think we should even hint at it?"

"I don't see any harm," Steele answered. "The Russians undoubtedly know the truth. They have agents everywhere. It might do a lot of good for American-British relations. Anyway, it would offset any fear that the saucers are Soviet weapons."

"Then you're not worried about that angle any more?"

Steele laughed. "No, but it had me going for a while. It was a big relief to find out the disks are British."

"What's the disks' ceiling?" I asked, abruptly.

"Oh - sixty thousand feet, at least," said Steele. After a moment he added quickly, "That's just a guess - they probably operate much higher. I didn't think to ask."

Before I hung up, he asked me what I thought, of the British explanation.

"It's certainly more plausible than the Soviet idea," I said. I thanked him for calling me, and put down the phone. I was tempted to point out the flaws in his story. But I didn't.

If he was sincere, it would be poor thanks for what he had told me. If he was trying to plant a fake explanation, it wouldn't hurt to let him think I'd swallowed it. When I saw Redell, I told him about Steele.

"It does look like an attempt to steer you away from the interplanetary answer," Redell agreed, "though he may be passing on a tip he believes."

"You think there could be any truth in the British story?"

"Would the British risk a hundred-foot disk crashing in some American city?" said Redell. "No remote control is perfect, and neither is a detonator system. By some freak accident, a disk might come down in a place like Chicago, and then blow up. I just can't see the British - any more than ourselves - letting huge unpiloted missiles go barging around the world, flying along airways and over cities. Certainly, they could have automatic devices to make them veer away from airliners - but what if a circuit failed?"

"I go along with that," I said.

"I don't say the British don't have some long-range missiles," Redell broke in. "Every big nation has a guided-missile project. But no guided missile on earth can explain the Mantell case and the others we've discussed."

I showed him the material I had on the Nazi disk experiments. Redell skimmed through it and nodded.

"I can tell you a little more," he said. "Some top Nazi scientists were convinced we were being observed by space visitors. They'd searched all the old reports. Some sighting over Germany set them off about 1940. That's what I was told. I think that's where they first got the idea of trying out oval and circular airfoils.

"Up to then, nobody was interested. The rotation idea uses the same principle as the helicopter, but nobody had even followed that through. The Nazis went to work on the disks. They also began to rush space-exploration plans - the orbiting satellite idea. I think they realized these space ships were using some great source of power we hadn't discovered on earth. I believe that's what they were after - that power secret. If they'd succeeded, they'd have owned the world. As it was, that space project caused them to leap ahead of everybody with rockets."

When I asked Redell how he thought the space ships were powered, he shrugged.

"Probably cosmic rays hold the answer. Their power would be even greater than atomic power. There's another source I've heard mentioned, but most people scoff at it. That's the use of electromagnetic fields in space. The earth has its magnetic field, of course, and so does the sun. Probably all planets do.

"There's a man named Fernand Roussel who wrote a book called The Unifying Principle of Physical Phenomena, about 1943. He goes into the electromagnetic-field theory. If he's right, then there must be some way to tap this force and go from one planet to another without using any fuel. You'd use your first planet's magnetic field to start you off and then coast through space until you got into the field of the next planet. At least, that's how I understand it. But you'd be safer sticking to atomic power. That's been proved."

Most of our conversations had been keyed to the technical side of the flying-saucer problem. But before I left this time, I asked Redell how the thought of space visitors affected him.

"Oh, at first I had a queer feeling about it," he answered. "But once you accept it, it's like anything else. You get used to the idea."

"One thing bothers me," I said. "When I try to picture them, I keep remembering the crazy-looking things in some of the comics. What do you suppose they're really like?"

"I've thought about it for months." Redell slowly shook his head. "I haven't the slightest idea."

CHAPTER XIV

THAT EVENING, after my talk with Redell, the question kept coming back in my mind.

What were they like? And what were they doing here?

From the long record of sightings, it was possible to get an answer to the second question. Observation of the earth followed a general pattern. According to the reports, Europe, the most populated area, had been more closely observed than the rest of the globe until about 1870. By this time, the United States, beginning to rival Europe in industrial progress, had evidently become of interest to the space-ship crews.

From then on, Europe and the Western Hemisphere, chiefly North America, shared the observers' attention. The few sightings reported at other points around the world indicate an occasional check-up on the earth in general. Apparently World War I had not greatly concerned the space observers. One reason might be that our aerial operations were still at a relatively low altitude.

But World War II had drawn more attention, and this had obviously increased from 1947 up to the present time. Our atomic-bomb explosions and the V-2 high-altitude experiments might be only coincidence, but I could think of no other development that might seriously concern dwellers on other planets.

It was a strange thing to think of some far-off race keeping track of the earth's progress. If Redell was right, it might even have started in prehistoric time; a brief survey, perhaps once a century or even further spaced, then gradually more frequent observation as cities appeared on the earth.

Somewhere on a distant planet there would be records of that long survey. I wondered how our development would appear to that far-advanced race. They would have seen the slow sailing ships, the first steamships, the lines of steel tracks that carried our first trains.

Watching for our first aircraft, they would see the drifting balloons that seemed an aerial miracle when the Montgolfiers first succeeded. More than a century later, they would have noted the slow, clumsy airplanes of the early 1900's. From our gradual progress to the big planes and bombers of today, they could probably chart our next steps toward the stratosphere - and then space.

During the last two centuries, they would have watched a dozen wars, each one fiercer than the last, spreading over the globe. Adding up all the things they had seen, they could draw an accurate picture of man, the earth creature, and the increasingly fierce struggle between the earth races.

The long survey held no sign of menace. If there had been a guiding purpose of attack and destruction, it could have been carried out years ago. It was almost certain that any planet race able to traverse space would have the means for attack.

More than once, during this investigation, I had been asked: "If the saucers are interplanetary, why haven't they landed here? Why haven't their crews tried to make contact with us?"

There was always the possibility that the planet race or races could not survive on earth, or that their communications did not include the methods that we used. But I found that hard to believe. Such a superior race would certainly be able to master our radio operations, or anything else that we had developed, in a fairly short time. And it should be equally simple to devise some means of survival on earth, just as we were already planning special suits and helmets for existence on the moon. During a talk with a former Intelligence officer, I got a key to the probable explanation.

"Why don't you just reverse it - list what we intend to do when we start exploring space? That'll give you the approximate picture of what visitors to the earth would be doing."

Naturally, all the details of space plans have not been worked out, but the general plan is clear. After the first successful earth satellites, we will either attempt a space base farther out or else launch a moon rocket. Probably many round trips to the moon will be made before going farther in space.

Which planet will be explored first, after the moon?

According to Air Force reports, it is almost a certainty that planets outside the solar system are inhabited. But because of the vast distances involved, expeditions to our neighboring planets may be tried before the more formidable journeys. More than one prominent astronomer believes that life, entirely different from our own, may exist on some solar planets. Besides Mars, Jupiter, and Venus, there are five more that, like the earth, revolve around the sun.

One of the prominent authorities is Dr. H. Spencer Jones, Astronomer Royal. In his book Life on Other Worlds, Dr. Jones points out that everything about us is the result of changing processes, begun millenniums ago and still going on. We cannot define life solely in our own terms; it can exist in unfamiliar forms.

"It is conceivable," Dr. Jones states in his book, "that we could have beings, the cells of whose bodies contained silicon instead of the carbon which is an essential constituent of our cells and of all other living cells on the earth. And that because of this essential difference between the constitution of those cells and the cells of which animal and plant life on the earth are built up, they might be able to exist at temperatures so high that no terrestrial types of life could survive."

According to Dr. Jones, then, life could be possible on worlds hotter and drier than ours; it could also exist on a very much colder one, such as Mars.

Even if a survey of the sun's planets proved fruitless, it would decide the question of their being populated. Also, it would provide valuable experience for the much longer journeys into space.

No one expects such a survey until we have a space vehicle able to make the round trip. One-way trips would tell us nothing, even if volunteers offered to make such suicidal journeys.

The most probable step will be to launch a space vehicle equipped with supplies for a long time, perhaps a year or two, within the solar system. Since Mars has been frequently mentioned as a source of the flying saucers, let's assume it would be the first solar-system planet to be explored from the earth.

As the space ship neared Mars, it could be turned to circle the planet in an orbit, just like our planned earth satellite vehicle. Once in this orbit, it could circle indefinitely without using fuel except to correct its course.

From this space base, unmanned remote-control "observer" units with television "eyes" or other transmitters would be sent down to survey the planet at close range. If it then seemed fairly safe, a manned unit could be released to make a more thorough check-up.

Such preliminary caution would be imperative. Our explorers would have no idea of what awaited them. The planet might be uninhabited. It might be peopled by a fiercely barbarous race unaware of civilization as we know it. Or it might have a civilization far in advance of ours.

The explorers would first try to get a general idea of the whole planet. Then they would attempt to examine the most densely populated areas, types of armature, any aircraft likely to attack them. Combing the radio spectrum, they would pick up and record sounds and signals in order to decipher the language.

As on earth, they might hear a hodgepodge of tongues. The next step would be to select the most technically advanced nation, listen in, and try to learn its language, or record it for deciphering afterward on earth.

Our astronomers already have analyzed Mars's atmosphere, but the explorers would have to confirm their reports, to find out whether the atmosphere at the surface would support their lungs if they landed. The easiest way would be to send down manned or unmanned units with special apparatus to scoop in atmosphere samples. Later analysis would tell whether earthlings would need oxygen-helmet suits such as we plan to use on the moon.

But before risking flight at such low altitudes, the explorers would first learn everything possible about the planet's aircraft, if any. They would try to determine their top ceiling, maximum speed, maneuverability, and if possible their weapons. Mitch of this could be done by sending down remote-control "observer" disks, or whatever type we decide to use. A manned unit might make a survey at night, or in daytime with clouds nearby to shield it. By hovering over the planet's aircraft bases, the explorers could get most of the picture, and also decide whether the bases were suitable for their own use later.

It might even be necessary to lure some Martian aircraft into pursuit of our units, to find out their performance. But our explorers would above all avoid any sign of hostility; they would hastily. withdraw to show they had no warlike intentions.

If the appearance of our observer units and manned craft caused too violent reactions on the planet, the explorers would withdraw to their orbiting space vehicle and either wait for a lull or else start the long trip back home. Another interplanetary craft from the earth might take its place later to resume periodic surveys.

In this way, a vast amount of information could be collected without once making contact with the strange race. If they seemed belligerent or uncivilized, we would probably end our survey and check on the next possibly inhabited planet. If we found they were highly civilized, we would undoubtedly attempt later contact. But it might take a long time, decades of observation and analysis, before we were ready for that final step.

We might find a civilization not quite so advanced as ours. It might not yet have developed radio and television. We would then have no way of getting a detailed picture, learning the languages, or communicating with. the Martians. Analysis of their atmosphere might show a great hazard to earthlings, one making it impossible to land or requiring years of research to overcome. There might be other obstacles beyond our present understanding.

This same procedure would apply to the rest of the solar-system planets and to more distant systems. Since Wolf 359 is the nearest star outside our system that is likely to have inhabited planets, one of these planets would probably be listed as the first to explore in far-distant space. It would be a tremendous undertaking, unless the speed of light can be exceeded in space. Since Wolf 359 is eight light-years from the earth, even if a space ship traveled at the theoretical maximum - just under 186,00 miles a second - it would take over sixteen years for the round trip. Detailed observation of the planet would add to this period.

If we assume half that speed - which would still be an incredible attainment with our present knowledge - our space explorers would have to dedicate at least thirty-two years to the hazardous, lonely round trip. However, there has never been a lack of volunteers for grand undertakings in the history of man.

It is quite possible that in our survey of the solar-system planets we would find some inhabited, but not advanced enough to be of interest to us. Periodically, we might make return visits to note their progress. Meantime, our astronomers would watch these planets, probably developing new, higher powered telescopes for the purpose, to detect any signs of unusual activity. Any tremendous explosion on a planet would immediately concern us.

Such an explosion, on Mars, was reported by astronomers on January 16, 1950. The cause and general effects are still being debated. Sadao Saeki, the Japanese astronomer who first reported it at Osaka, believes it was of volcanic nature.

The explosion created a cloud over an area about seven hundred miles in diameter and forty miles high. It was dull gray with a yellowish tinge and a different color from the atmospheric phenomena customarily seen near Mars. Saeki believes the blast might have destroyed any form of life existing on the planet, but even though the telescopic camera recorded a violent explosion, other authorities do not believe the planet was wrecked. The canals first discovered on Mars by Giovanni Schiaparelli, about 1877, are still apparent on photographs.

Mars is now being carefully watched by astronomers. If there are more of the strange explosions, the planet will be scanned constantly for some clue to their nature.

If a mysterious explosion on Mars, or any other planet, were found of atomic origin, it would cause serious concern on earth. Suppose for a moment that it happened many years from now, when we will have succeeded in space explorations. At this time, let us assume our explorers have found that Mars is experimenting with high-altitude rockets; some of them have been seen, rising at tremendous speed, in the upper atmosphere of Mars.

Then comes this violent explosion. A scientific analysis of the cloud by astrophysicists here on earth proves it was of atomic origin.

The first reaction would undoubtedly be an immediate resurvey of Mars. As quickly as possible, we would establish an orbiting space base - out of range of Martian rockets - and try to find how far they had advanced with atomic bombs.

Samples of the Martian atmosphere would be collected and analyzed for telltale radiation. Observer units would be flown over the planet, with instruments to locate atom-bomb plants and possibly uranium deposits. The rocket-launching bases would also come under close observation. We would try to learn how close the scientists were to escaping the pull of gravity. Since Mars's gravity is much less than the earth's, the Martians would not have so far to progress before succeeding in space travel.

The detailed survey by our space-base observers would probably show that there was no immediate danger to the earth. It might take one hundred years - perhaps five hundred - before the Martians could be a problem. Eventually, the time would come when Mars would send out space-ship explorers. They would undoubtedly discover that the earth was populated with a technically advanced civilization. Any warlike ideas they had in mind could be quickly ended by a show of our superior spacecraft and our own atomic weapons - probably far superior to any on Mars. It might even be possible that by then we would have finally outlawed war; if so, a promise to share the peaceful benefits of our technical knowledge might be enough to bring Martian leaders into line.

Regardless of our final decision, we would certainly keep a lose watch on Mars - or any other planet that seemed a possible threat.

Now, if our space-exploration program is just reversed, it will give a reasonable picture of how visitors from space might go about investigating the earth. Such an investigation would tie in with the general pattern of authentic flying-saucer reports:

1. World-wide sightings at long intervals up to the middle of the nineteenth century.

2. Concentration on Europe, as the most advanced section of the globe, until late in the nineteenth century.

3. Frequent surveys of America in the latter part of the nineteenth century, as we began to develop industrially, with cities springing up across the land.

4. Periodic surveys of both America and Europe during the gradual development of aircraft, from the early 1900's up to World War II.

5. An increase of observation during World War II, after German V-2's were launched up into the stratosphere.

6. A steadily increasing survey after our atomic-bomb explosions in New Mexico, Japan, Bikini, and Eniwetok.

7. A second spurt of observations following atom-bomb explosions in Soviet Russia.

8. Continuing observations of the earth at regular intervals, with most attention concentrated on the United States, the present leader in atomic weapons. (Saucers have been reported seen over the Soviet Union, but the number is unknown. There is some evidence that Russia has an investigative unit similar to Project "Saucer.")

There are other points of similarity to the program of American space exploration that I have outlined. Most of the extremely large saucers have been at high altitudes, some of them many miles above the earth. At that height, a space ship would be in no danger from our planes and antiaircraft guns and rockets. The smaller disks and the mystery lights have been seen at low altitudes. Occasionally a larger saucer has been seen to approach the earth briefly, as at Lockbourne Air Force Base, at Bethel, Alabama, at Macon and Montgomery, and other places. It has been suggested that this was for the purpose of securing atmospheric samples. It could also be to afford personal observation by the crews.

The numerous small disks seen in the first part of the scare, in 1947, fit the pattern for preliminary and close observation by remote-controlled observer units. As the scare increased, the daytime sightings decreased for a while, and mystery lights began to be seen more often. This apparent desire to avoid unfavorable attention could have been caused by our pilots' repeated attempts to chase the strange flying objects.

Authentic reports have described sightings; over the following Air Force bases: Chanute, Newark, Andrews, Hickam, Robbins, Godman, Clark, Fairfield Suisan, Davis-Monthan, Harmon, Wright-Patterson, Holloman, Clinton County Air Force Base, and air bases in Alaska, Germany, and the Azores. Saucers have also been sighted over naval air stations at Dallas, Alameda, and Key West, and from the station at Seattle. They have been reported maneuvering over the White Sands Proving Ground, over areas containing atomic developments, above the Muroc Air Base testing area, and over the super-secret research base near Albuquerque.

Several times saucers have paced both military and civil aircraft; their actions strongly indicate deliberate encounters to learn our planes' speed and performance.

It seems obvious that both the planes and the bases were being observed, and in some cases photographed by remote-control units or manned space ships.

Although I thought it improbable that the location of our uranium deposits would be of interest to space men, a Washington official told me it would be relatively simple to detect the ore areas with airborne instruments.

"The Geological Survey has already developed special Geiger counters for planes," he told me. "They had a little trouble from cosmic-ray noise. They finally had to cover the Geigers with lead shields. Whenever an important amount of radiation is present in the ground, the plane crew gets a signal, and they spot the place on their map. It's a quick way of locating valuable deposits."

When I told him what I had in mind, he suggested an angle I had not considered.

"Mind you," he said, "I'm not completely sold on the interplanetary answer. But assuming it's correct that we're being observed, I can think of a stronger reason than fear of some distant attack. Some atomic scientists say that a super-atomic bomb, or several set off at once, could knock the earth out of its orbit. It sounds fantastic, but so is the A-bomb. It's just possible that some solar-planet race discovered the dangers long ago. They would have good reason to worry if they found we were on that same track. There may be some other atomic weapon we don't suspect, even worse than the A-bomb, one that could destroy the earth and seriously affect other planets."

At the time, I thought this was just idle speculation. But since then, several atomic scientists have confirmed this official's suggestion. One of these was Dr. Paul Elliott, a nuclear physicist who worked on the A-bomb during the war.

According to Dr. Elliott, if several hydrogen bombs

were exploded simultaneously at a high altitude, it could speed up the earth's rotation or change its orbit. He based his statement on the rate of energy the earth receives from the sun, a rate equal to some four pounds of hydrogen exploded every second. Still other atomic scientists have said that H-bomb explosions might even knock a large chunk out of the earth, with unpredictable results.

A dramatic picture of what might happen if the earth were forced far out of its orbit is indicated in the much-discussed book Worlds in Collision, by Dr. Immanuel Velikovsky, recently published by Macmillan. After many years of research, Dr. Velikovsky presents strong evidence that the planet Venus, when still a comet resulting from eruption from a larger planet, moved erratically about the sky and violently disturbed both the earth and Mars.

When the comet approached the earth, our planet was forced out of its orbit, according to Worlds in Collision. For a time, the world was on the brink of destruction. Quoting many authentic ancient records, including the Quiché manuscript of the Mayas, the Ipuwer papyrus of the Egyptians, and the Visiddhi-Magga of the Buddhists, Dr. Velikovsky describes the cataclysm that took place. "The face of the earth changed," he writes in his book. The details, reinforced by the Zend-Avesta of the Persians, tell of tremendous hurricanes, of a major upheaval in the earth's surface, of oceans rushing over many parts of the land, while rivers were driven from their beds. Some of the events in this period are mentioned in the Bible.

Professor Horace M. Kallen, former dean of the New School of Social Research, strongly endorses Dr.

Velikovsky's statements: "It is my belief that Velikovsky has supported his theses with substantial evidence and made an effective and persuasive argument."

Many other authorities endorse this work, which is documented with impressive references. But even if this particular account is not accepted, all astronomers agree that the effect of a comet passing near the earth would be appalling. Worlds in Collision states that Mars, like the earth, was pulled out of its orbit by the comet's erratic passage. It may be that this near disaster to the earth and Mars is known on other solar planets, or remembered on Mars itself, if the planet is inhabited.

The possibility of super-bomb explosions on the earth understandably disturb any dwellers on other solar-system planets.

This may be what was back of the Project "Saucer" statement on the probable motives of any visitors from space. I mentioned this Air Force statement in an earlier chapter, but it may be of interest to repeat it at this time. The comment appeared in a confidential analysis of Intelligence reports, in the formerly secret Project "Saucer" document, "Report on Unidentified Aerial and Celestial Objects." It reads as follows:

"Such a civilization might observe that on earth we now have atomic bombs and are fast developing rockets. In view of the past history of mankind, they should be alarmed. We should therefore expect at this time above all to behold such visitations.

"Since the acts of mankind most easily observed from

a distance are A-bomb explosions, we should expect some relation to obtain between the time of the A-bomb explosions, the time at which the space ships are seen, and the time required for such ships to arrive from and return to home base."

CHAPTER XV

IT was early in October 1949 when I finished the reversal of our space-exploration plans. I spent the next two days running down a sighting report from a town in Pennsylvania. Like three or four other tips that had seemed important at first, it turned out to be a dud.

When I got back home, I found Ken Purdy had been trying to reach me. I phoned him at True, and he asked me to fly up to New York the next day.

"I've just heard there's another magazine working on the saucer story," he told me.

"Who is it?" I said.

"I don't know yet. It may be just a rumor, but we can't take a chance. We've got to get this in the January book."

That night I gathered up all the material. It looked hopeless to condense it into one article, and I knew that Purdy had even more investigators' reports waiting for me in New York. Flying up the next morning, I suddenly thought of a talk I'd had with an air transport official. It was in Washington; I had just told him about the investigation.

"If they are spacemen," he said, "they'd probably have a hard time figuring out this country by listening to our broadcasts. Imagine tuning in soap operas, 'The Lone Ranger,' and a couple of crime yarns, along with newscasts about strikes and murders and the cold war. They might pick up some of those kid programs about rocket ships. A few days of listening to that stuff - well, it would give them one hell of a picture."

Except for some hoax reports, this was the first funny suggestion I'd had about the spacemen. But now, thinking seriously about it, I realized he had an important point. It was possible that men from another planet might have to reorient even their way of thinking to understand the earth's ways. It would not be automatic, despite their superior technical progress. Evolution might have produced basic differences in their understanding of life. Humor, for instance, might be totally lacking in their make-up.

What would they be like?

I'd tried to imagine how they might look, without getting anywhere. Dr. H. Spencer Jones hadn't helped much with his Life on Other Worlds. I couldn't begin to visualize beings with totally different cells, perhaps able to take terrific heat or bitter cold as merely normal weather.

There were all kinds of possibilities. If they lived on Mars, for instance, perhaps they couldn't take the heavier gravity of the earth. They might be easily subject to our diseases, especially if they had destroyed disease germs on their planet - a natural step for an advanced race.

It was possible, I knew, that the spacemen might look grotesque to us. But I clung to a Stubborn feeling that they would resemble man. That came, of course, from an inborn feeling of man's superiority over all living things. It carried over into a feeling that any thinking, intelligent being, whether on Mars or Wolf 359's planets, should have evolved in the same form.

I gave up trying to imagine how the spacemen might look. There was simply nothing to go on. But there were strong indications of how they thought and reacted. Certain qualities were plainly evident.

Intelligence
- No one could dispute that. It took a high order of mentality to construct and operate a space ship.

Courage
- It would take brave men to face the hazards of space.

Curiosity
- Without this quality, they would never have thought to explore far-distant planets.

There were other qualities that seemed almost equally certain. These spacemen apparently lacked belligerence; there had been no sign of hostility through all the years. They were seemingly painstaking and extremely methodical.

It was still not much of a picture. But somehow, it was encouraging.

Glancing down from the plane's window, I thought:

How does this look to them? Our farms, our cities, the railroads there below; the highways, with the speeding cars and trucks; the winding river, and far off to the right, the broad stretch of the Atlantic.

What would they think of America?

Manhattan came into sight, as the pilot let down for the landing. An odd thought popped into my mind. How would a spaceman react if he saw a Broadway show?

Not long before, I had seen South Pacific. I could still hear Ezio Pinza's magnificent voice as he sang "Some Enchanted Evening."

Was music a part of spacemen's lives, or would it be something new and strange, perhaps completely distasteful?

They might live and think on a coldly intelligent level, without a touch of what we know as emotion. To them, our lives might seem meaningless and dull. We ourselves might appear grotesque in form.

But in their progress, there must have been struggle, trial and error, some feeling of triumph at success. Surely these would be emotional forces, bound to reflect in the planet races. Perhaps, in spite of some differences, we would find a common bond - the bond of thinking, intelligent creatures trying to better themselves.

The airliner landed and taxied in to unload.

As I went down the gangway I suddenly realized something. My last vague fear was gone.

It had not been a personal fear of the visitors from space. It had been a selfish fear of the impact on my life. I realized that now.

It might be a long time before they would try to make contact. But I had a conviction that when it came, it would be a peaceful mission, not an ultimatum. It could even be the means of ending wars on earth.

But I had been conditioned to this thing. I had had six months of preparation, six months to go from complete skepticism to slow, final acceptance.

What if it had been thrown at me in black headlines?

Even a peaceful contact by beings from another planet would profoundly affect the world. The story in True might play an important part in that final effect. Carefully done, it could help prepare Americans for the official disclosure.

But if it weren't done right, we might be opening a Pandora's box.

CHAPTER XVI

THAT MORNING, at True, we made the final decisions on how to handle the story. Using the evidence of the Mantell case, the Chiles-Whitted report, Gorman's mystery-light encounter, and other authentic cases, along with the records of early sightings, we would state our main conclusion: that the flying saucers were interplanetary.

In going over the mass of reports, Purdy and I both realized that a few sightings did not fit the space-observer pattern. Most of these reports came from the southwest states, where guided-missile experiments were going on.

Purdy agreed with Paul Redell that any long-range tests would be made over the sea or unpopulated areas, with every attempt at secrecy.

"They might make short-range tests down there in New Mexico and Arizona-maybe over Texas," he said. "But they'd never risk killing people by shooting the things all over the country."

"They've already set up a three-thousand-mile range for the longer runs," I added. "It runs from Florida into the South Atlantic. And the Navy missiles at Point Mugu are launched out over the Pacific. Any guided missiles coming down over settled areas would certainly be an accident. Besides all that, no missile on earth can explain these major cases."

Purdy was emphatic about speculating on our guided-missile research.

"Suppose you analyzed these minor cases that look like missile tests. You might accidentally give away something important, like their range and speeds. Look what the Russians did with the A-bomb hints Washington let out."

It was finally decided that we would briefly mention the guided missiles, along with the fact that the armed services had flatly denied any link with the saucers.

"After all, interplanetary travel is the main story," said Purdy. "And the Mantell case alone proves we've been observed from space ships, even without the old records."

The question of the story's impact worried both of us. Public acceptance of intelligent life on other planets would affect almost every phase of our existence-business, defense planning, philosophy, even religion. Of course, the immediate effect was more important. Personally, I thought that most Americans could take even an official announcement without too much trouble. But I could be wrong.

"The only yardstick - and that's not much good - is that 'little men' story," said Purdy. "A lot of people have got excited about it, but they seem more interested than scared."

The story of the "little men from Venus" had been circulating for some time. In the usual version, two flying saucers had come down near our southwest border. In the space craft were several oddly dressed men, three feet high. All of them were dead; the cause was usually given as inability to stand our atmosphere. The Air Force was said to have hushed up the story, so that the public could be educated gradually to the truth. Though it had all the earmarks of a well-thought-out hoax, many newspapers had repeated the story. It had even been broadcast as fact on several radio newscasts. But there had been no signs of public alarm.

"It looks as if people have come a long way since that Orson Welles scare," I said to Purdy.

"But there isn't any menace in this story," he objected. "The crews were reported dead, so everybody got the idea that spacemen couldn't live if they landed. What if a space ship should suddenly come down over a big city - say New York - low enough for millions of people to see it?"

"it might cause a stampede," I said,

Purdy snorted. "it would be a miracle if it didn't, unless people had been fully prepared. if we do a straight fact piece, just giving the evidence, it will start the ball rolling. People at least will be thinking about it."

Before I left for Washington, I told Purdy of my last visit to the Pentagon. I had informed Air Force press relations officials of True's intention to publish the space-travel answer. There had been no attempt to dissuade me. And I had been told once again that there was no security involved; that Project "Saucer" had found nothing threatening the safety of America.

At this time I had also asked if Project "Saucer" files were now available. The Wright Field unit, I was told, still was a classified project, both its files and its photographs secret. This had been the first week in October.

When I asked if there was any other information on published cases, the answer again was negative. The April 27th report, according to Press Branch officials, was still an accurate statement of Air Force opinions and policies. So far as they knew, no other explanations had be n found for the unidentified saucers.

'I in absolutely convinced now," I told Purdy, "that here's an official policy to let the thing leak out. It explains why Forrestal announced our Earth Satellite Vehicle program, years before we could even start to build it. It also would explain those Project 'Saucer' hints in the April report."

"I think we're being used as a trial balloon," Purdy said thoughtfully. "We've let them know what we're doing. If they'd wanted to stop us, the Air Force could easily have done it. All they'd have to do would be call us in, give us the dope off the record, and tell us it was a patriotic duty to keep still. Just the way they did about uranium and atomic experiments during the war."

He still did not have the name of the other magazine supposed to be working on the saucers. But it seemed a reliable tip (it later proved to be true), and from then on we worked under high pressure.

In writing the article, I used only the most authentic recent sightings; all of the cases were in the Air Force reports. When it came to the Mantell case, I stuck to published estimates of the strange object's size; a mysterious ship 250 to 300 feet in diameter was startling enough. At first, I chose Mars to illustrate our space explorations. But Mars had been associated with the Orson Welles stampede. Most discussions of the planet had a menacing note, perhaps because of its warlike name.

In the end, I switched to a planet of Wolf 359. The thought of those eight light-years would have a comforting effect on any nervous readers. The chance of any mass visitation would seem remote, if not impossible. But it would still put across the space-travel story.

As finally revised, the article, written under my byline, stated the following points as the conclusions reached by True:

1. For the past 175 years, the earth has been under systematic close-range examination by living, intelligent observers from another planet.

2. The intensity of this observation, and the frequency of the visits to the earth's atmosphere, have increased markedly during the past two years.

3. The vehicles used for this observation and for interplanetary transport by the explorers have been classed as follows: Type I, a small, nonpilot-carrying disk-shaped craft equipped with some form of television or impulse transmitter; Type II, a very large, metallic, disk-shaped aircraft operating on the

helicopter principle; Type III, a dirigible-shaped, wingless aircraft that, in the Earth's atmosphere, operates in conformance with the Prandtl theory of lift.

4. The discernible patterns of observation and exploration shown by the so-called flying disks varies in no important particular from well-developed American plans for the exploration of space, expected to come to fruition within the next fifty years. There is reason to believe, however, that some other race of thinking beings is a matter of two and a quarter centuries ahead of us.

Following these points, I added a brief comment on the possibility of guided missiles, adding that the Air Force had convincingly denied this as an explanation of any sightings. As Purdy had suggested, I carefully omitted ten minor cases that I thought might be linked with guided-missile research. If disclosing the facts about space travel helped to divert attention from any secret tests, so much the better.

"True accepts the official denial of any secret device," I stated, "because the weight of the evidence, especially the world-wide sightings, does not support such a belief."

Most readers, of course, would know that some guided-missile experiments were going on, and that True was fully aware of it. But our main purpose would be achieved.

The fact that the earth had been observed by beings from another planet would be fully presented. Some readers, of course, would reject even the fact that the saucers existed. Others would cling to the idea that they were of earthly origin. But the mass of evidence would make most readers think. At the very least, it would plant one strong suggestion: that we, men and women of the earth, are not the only intelligent species in the universe. When the article was finished, it was tried out on True's staff, then on a picked group that had not known about the investigation. One editor summed up the average opinion:

"It will cause a lot of discussion, but the way it's written, it shouldn't start any panic."

The January issue, in which the story ran, was due on the stands shortly after Christmas. With my family, I had gone to Ottumwa, Iowa, to spend the holidays with my mother and sister. While I was there, the story broke unexpectedly on radio networks.

Frank Edwards, Mutual network newscaster, led off the radio comment. He was followed by Walter Winchell, Lowell Thomas, Morgan Beatty, and most of the other radio commentators. The wire services quickly picked it up; some papers ran front-page stories.

The publicity was far more than I had expected. I phoned a reporter in Washington whose beat includes the Pentagon.

"The Air Force is running around in circles," he told me. "They knew your story was due, but nobody thought it would raise such a fuss. I think they're scared of hysteria. They're getting a barrage of wires and telephone calls."

That night, as I was packing to rush back east , he

called with the latest news.

"They're going to deny the whole thing," he said. "But' I heard one Press Branch guy say it might not be enough - they're trying to figure some way to knock it down fast."

Next day, while changing trains at Chicago, I saw the Air Force statement. The press release was dated December 27, 1949. Without mentioning True, the Air Force flatly denied having any evidence that flying saucers exist. After examining 375 reports, the release said, Project "Saucer" had found that they were caused by:

1. Misinterpretation of various conventional objects.

2. A mild form of mass hysteria or "war nerves."

3. Individuals who fabricate such reports to perpetrate a hoax or to seek publicity.

Evaluation of the reports of unidentified flying objects, said the Air Force, demonstrates that they constitute no direct threat to the national security of the United States.

Then came the clincher: Project "Saucer," said the Air Force, had been discontinued, now that all the reports had been explained.

It was plain that the release had been hastily prepared. It completely contradicted the detailed Project "Saucer" report, issued eight months before, that had called for constant vigilance, after admitting that most important cases were unsolved. Anyone familiar with the situation would see the discrepancy at once.

From Washington I flew to New York, where I found True in a turmoil. Long-distance calls were pouring in. Letters on flying saucers had swamped the mail room. Reporters were hounding Purdy for more information.

A hurried analysis of the first hundred letters showed a trend that later mail confirmed. Less than 5 per cent of the readers ridiculed the article. Between 15 and 20 per cent said they were not convinced; a few of these admitted they could not refute the evidence. About half the readers accepted the possibility; most of these said they saw no reason why other planets should not be inhabited. The remainder, between 25 and 30 per cent, said they were completely convinced.

Even the disbelievers asked for more information. The intelligence level of the average letter was gratifyingly high. Comments came from scientists, engineers, airline and private pilots, college professors, officers of the armed services, and a wide variety of others - including far more women than True's readership usually includes.

Several confidential tips had come in when I arrived. Most of them were from usually reputable sources. We were given evidence that Project "Saucer" was still in operation; since its true code name was not "Saucer," it could be continued without violating the Air Force press release. This same information was received from a dozen sources within the next two weeks. We were also told that there had been 722 cases, instead of 375.

Meantime, a number of astronomers had come out with

statements, pro and con. One of these was Dr. Dean B. McLaughlin, of the University of Michigan.

"No one knows what the saucers are as yet," Dr. McLaughlin said. "They could be anything, and I'm willing to be convinced once the evidence is presented."

Dr. Bart J. Bok of Harvard was on the fence: "After all," he said, "all sort of things float around in space. But I'm not convinced the saucers are anything apart from the earth."

Another Harvard astronomer, Dr. Armin J. Deutsch, took an oblique poke at True and me. "I don't think anyone - and that includes astronomers - knows enough about them to reach any conclusions."

After this came the comment of Dr. Carl F. von Weizacker - that billions of stars may have planets, and many could be inhabited.

Within a few days we had a huge stack of clippings, some supporting True, some deriding us. In the midst of all this, I read scientists' comments on Einstein's new unified-field theory, which had been printed about the time True appeared on the stands. A discussion by Lincoln Barnett, author of The Universe and Dr. Einstein, explained the basic premise - that gravitation and electromagnetic force are inseparable. As I read it, I thought of what Redell had said. If gravitation were a manifestation of electromagnetic force, was it possible that an advanced race had found a way - as unique as splitting the atom - to offset gravity and utilize that force?

It was during these first tense days that we ran down the White Sands story. This also ended another puzzle - the identity of the magazine that we had feared might scoop us.

The race had been closer than we knew. The editors of a national magazine had learned of Commander McLaughlin and the sightings at White Sands. Two of the staff had carefully investigated the details. Convinced that the report was accurate, they had planned to run the story in an early issue.

Since True had appeared first with the space-travel story, the editors agreed to release the McLaughlin report for use in our March issue. The basic facts were in close agreement with what Redell had told me.

The ellipsoid-shaped saucer had been tracked at a height of 56 miles, its speed 5 miles per second. This was 18,000 miles per hour, even faster than Redell had said. The strange craft, 105 feet in length, had climbed as swiftly as Marvin Miles had described it - an increase in altitude of about 25 miles in 10 seconds.

Commander McLaughlin stated in his article that he was convinced the object was a space ship from another planet, operated by animate, intelligent beings. He also described two small circular objects, about twenty inches in diameter, that streaked up beside a Navy high-altitude missile. After maneuvering around it for a moment, both disks accelerated, passed the fast-moving Navy missile, and disappeared.

It is Commander McLaughlin's opinion that the saucers come from Mars. Pointing out that Mars was in a good position to see our surface on July 16, 1945, he believes that the flash of the first A-bomb, at Alamogordo Base, a point not far from White Sands, was caught by powerful telescopes.

During the first week of January, I appeared on "We, the People," with Lieutenant George Gorman. When I saw Gorman, before rehearsals, he seemed oddly constrained. I had a feeling that he had been warned about talking freely. During rehearsals, he changed his lines in the script. When the writers argued over a point, Gorman told them:

"I can say only what was in my published report - nothing else."

The day before the broadcast, a program official told me they had been told to include the Air Force denial in the script. That afternoon I learned that the Air Force planned to monitor the broadcast.

Meantime, an A.P. story carried a new Air Force announcement. Formerly secret Project "Saucer" files would be opened to newsmen at the Pentagon, giving the answers to all the saucer reports.

Just after my return to Washington, I saw an I.N.S. story that was widely printed. It was an interview with Major Jerry Boggs, a Project "Saucer" Intelligence officer who served as liaison man between Wright Field and the Pentagon. Major Boggs had been asked for specific answers to the Mantell, Chiles-Whitted, and Gorman cases.

The answers he gave amazed me. I picked up the phone and called the Air Force Press Branch. After some delay, I was told that Major Boggs was being briefed for assignment to Germany. An interview would be almost impossible.

"He wasn't too busy to talk with I.N.S.," I said. "All I want is thirty minutes."

Later, Jack Shea, a civilian press official I had known for some time, arranged for the meeting. I was also to talk with General Sory Smith, Deputy Director for Air Information.

Major Jesse Stay, a Press Branch officer, took me to General Smith's office for the interview. Both Jesse and Jack Shea, pleasant, obliging chaps who had helped me in the past, tried earnestly to convince me the saucers didn't exist. Jesse was still trying when Major Boggs came in.

Boggs looked to be in his twenties, younger than I had expected. He was trim, well built, with a quietly alert face. Two rows of ribbons testified to his wartime service. When Jesse Stay introduced me, Boggs gave me a curiously searching look. It could have been merely his usual way of appraising people he met. But all through our talk, I had a strong feeling that he was on his guard.

I had written out some questions, but first I mentioned the I.N.S. story.

"Were you quoted correctly on the Mantell case?" I asked.

"Yes, I was." Major Boggs looked me squarely in the eye. "Captain Mantell was chasing the planet Venus."

It was so incredible that I shook my head. "Major, Venus; was practically invisible that day. We've checked with astronomers. Is that the official Air Force answer?"

"Yes, it is," Boggs said. His eyes never left my face. I glanced across at General Sory Smith, then back at the intelligence major.

"That's a flat contradiction of Project 'Saucer's' report. Last April, after they had checked for fifteen months, they said positively it was not Venus. It was still unidentified."

Boggs said, in a slow, unruffled voice, "They rechecked after that report."

"Why did they recheck, after fifteen months?" I asked him. "'They must have gone over those figures long before that, for errors."

If my question annoyed him, Boggs gave no sign.

There's no other possible answer," he said. "Mantell was chasing Venus."

CHAPTER XVII

FOR A MOMENT after Boggs's last answer, I had an impulse to end the interview. I had a feeling I was facing a sphinx - a quiet, courteous sphinx in an Air Force uniform.

I was sure now why Major Jerry Boggs had been chosen for his job, the all-important connecting link with the project at Wright Field. No one would ever catch this man off guard, no matter what secret was given him to conceal. And it was more than the result of Air Force Intelligence training. His manner, his voice carried conviction. He would have convinced anyone who had not carefully analyzed the Godman Field tragedy.

I made one more attempt. "Do the Godman Field witnesses - Colonel Hix and the rest - believe the Venus answer?"

"I haven't asked them," said Boggs, "so I couldn't say."

"What about the Chiles-Whitted case?" I asked. "You were quoted as saying they saw a meteor - a bolide that exploded in a shower of sparks."

"That's right," said Boggs.

"And Gorman was chasing a lighted balloon?"

Again the Intelligence major nodded. I pointed, out that all three of the cases mentioned had been listed as unidentified in the April report.

"They'd had those cases for months," I said. "What new facts did they learn?"

Boggs said calmly, "They just made a final analysis, and those were the answers."

We looked at each other a moment. Major Boggs patiently waited. I began to realize how a lawyer must feel with an imperturbable witness. And Boggs's unfailing courtesy began to make me embarrassed.

"Major," I said, "I hope you'll realize this is not a personal matter. As an Intelligence officer, if you're told to give certain answers - "

He smiled for the first time. "That's all right - but I'm not hiding a thing. There's just no such thing as a flying saucer, so far as we've found out."

"We've been told," I said, "that Project 'Saucer' isn't closed - that you just changed its code name."

"That's not so," Boggs said emphatically. "The contracts are ended, and all personnel transferred to other duty."

"Then the announcement wasn't caused by True's article?"

Both General Smith and Major Jesse Stay shook their

heads quickly. Boggs leaned forward, eyeing me earnestly.

"As a matter of fact, we'd finished the investigation months ago - around the end of August, or early in September. We just hadn't got around to announcing it."

"Last October," I said, "I was told the investigation was still going on. They said there were no new answers to the cases just mentioned."

"The Press Branch hadn't been informed yet," Boggs explained simply.

"It seems very strange to me," I said. "In April, the Air Force called for vigilance by the civilian population. It said the project was young, much of its work still under way."

Jesse Stay interrupted before Boggs could reply.

"Don, the Press Branch will have to take the blame for that. The report wasn't carefully checked. There were several loose statements in it."

This was an incredible statement. I was sure Jesse knew it.

"But the case reports you quoted came from Wright Field. As of April twenty-seventh, 1949, all the major cases were officially unsolved. Then in August or early September, the whole thing's cleaned up, from what Major Boggs says. That's pretty hard to believe."

No one answered that one. Major Boggs was waiting

politely for the next question. I picked up my list. The rest of the interview was in straight question-and-answer style:

Q. Do you know about the White Sands sightings in April 1948? The ones Commander R. B. McLaughlin has written up?

A. Yes, we checked the reports. We just don't believe them.

Q. One of the witnesses was Charles B. Moore, the director of the Navy cosmic-ray project at Minneapolis, He's considered a very reputable engineer. Did you know he confirms the first report - the one about the saucer 56 miles up, at a speed of eighteen thousand miles per hour.

A. Yes, I knew about him. We think he was mistaken, like the others.

Q. Mr. Moore says it was absolutely sure it was not hallucination. He says it should be carefully investigated.

A. We did investigate. We just don't believe they saw anything.

Q. Could I see the complete file on that case? Also on Mantell, Gorman, and the Eastern Airlines cases?

A. That's out of my province.

Q. If Project "Saucer" is ended, then all the files should be opened.

A. Well, the summaries have been cleared, and you can see them.

Q. No, I mean the actual files. Is there any reason I shouldn't see them?

A. There'd be a lot of material to search through. Each case has a separate book, and some of them are pretty bulky.

Q. There were 722 cases in all, weren't there?

A. No, nowhere near that.

Q. Then 375 is the total figure - I mean the number of cases Project "Saucer" listed?

A. There were a few more - something over four hundred. I don't know the exact figure.

Q. I've been told that Project "Saucer" had the Air Force put out a special order for pilots to chase flying saucers. Is that right?

A. Yes, that's right.

Q. Did that include National Guard pilots?

A. Yes, it did. When the project first started checking on saucers we were naturally anxious to get hold of one of the things. We told the pilots to do practically anything in reason, even if they had to grab one by the tail.

Q. Were any of those planes armed?

A. Only if they happened to have guns for some other mission, like gunnery practice.

Q. We've heard of one case where fighters chased a saucer to a high altitude. One of them emptied his guns at it.

A. You must mean that New Jersey affair. The plane was armed for another reason.

Q. No, I meant a case reported out at Luke Field. Three fighters took off, if the story sent us is correct. Apparently it made quite a commotion. That was back in 1945.

A. It might have happened. I don't know.

Q. What was this New Jersey case?

A. I'd rather not discuss any more cases without having the books here.

Q. Has Project "Saucer" released its secret pictures?

A. What pictures? There weren't any that amounted to anything. Maybe half a dozen. They didn't show anything, just spots on film or weather balloons at a distance.

Q. In the Kenneth Arnold case, didn't some forest rangers verify his report?

A. Well, there were some people who claimed they saw the same disks. But we found out later they'd heard about it on the radio.

Q. Didn't they draw some sketches that matched Arnold's?

A. I never heard about it.

Q. I'd like to go back to the Mantell case a second. If Venus was so bright - remember Mantell thought it was a huge metallic object - why didn't the pilot who made the search later on -

A. Well, it was Venus, that's positive. But I can't remember all the details without the case books.

Q. One more question, Major. Have any reports been received at Wright Field since Project "Saucer" closed? There was a case after that date, an airliner crew -

At this point, Major Jesse Stay broke in.

"It's all up to the local commanders now. If they want to receive reports of anything unusual, all right. And if they want to investigate them, that's up to each commander. But no Project 'Saucer' teams will check on reports. That's all ended."

There at the last, it had been a little. like a courtroom scene, and I was glad the interview was over. Major Boggs was unruffled as ever. I apologized for the barrage of questions, and thanked him for being so decent about it.

"It was interesting, getting your viewpoint," he said. He smiled, still the courteous sphinx, and went on out.

After Bogs had left, I talked with General Smith alone. I told him I was not convinced,

"I'd like to see the complete files on these cases I mentioned," I explained. "Also, I'd like to talk with the last commanding officer or senior Intelligence officer attached to Project 'Saucer.'"

"I'm not sure about the senior officer," General Smith answered. "He may have been detached already. But I don't see any reason why you can't see those files. I'll phone Wright Field and call you."

I was about to leave, but he motioned for me to sit down.

"I can understand how you feel about the Mantell report," General Smith said earnestly. "I knew Tommy Mantell very well. And Colonel Hix is a classmate of mine. I knew neither one was the kind to have hallucinations. That case got me, at first."

"You believe Venus is the true answer?" I asked him.

He seemed surprised. "It must be, if Wright Field says so."

When I went back to the Press Branch, I asked Jack Shea for the case-report summaries that Boggs had mentioned, He got them for me - two collections of loose-leaf mimeographed sheets enclosed in black binders. So these were the "secret files"!

Across the hall, in the press room, I opened one book at random. The first thing I saw was this:

"A meteorologist should compute the approximate energy required to evaporate as much cloud as shown in the incident 26 photographs."

Photographs.

Major Boggs had said there were no important pictures.

I tucked the binders under my arm and went out to my car. Perhaps these books hinted at more than Boggs had realized. But that didn't seem likely. As liaison man, he should know all the answers. I was almost positive that he did.

But I was equally sure they weren't the answers he had given me.

CHAPTER XVIII

THAT NIGHT I went through the Project "Saucer" summary of cases. It was a strange experience.

The first report I checked was the Mantell case. Nothing that Boggs had said had changed my firm opinion. I knew the answer was not Venus, and I was certain Boggs knew it, too.

The Godman Field incident was listed as Case 33. The report also touches on the Lockbourne Air Base sighting. As already described, the same mysterious object, or a similar one, was seen moving at five hundred miles an hour over Lockbourne Field. It was also sighted at other points in Ohio.

The very first sentence in Case 33 showed a determined attempt to explain away the object that Mantell chased:

"Detailed attention should be given to any possible astronomical body or phenomenon which might serve to identify the object or objects."

(Some of the final Project report on Mantell has been given in an earlier chapter. I am repeating a few paragraphs below, to help in weighing Major Boggs's answer.)

These are official statements of the Project astronomer:

"On January 7, 1948, Venus was less than half its full brilliance. However, under exceptionally good atmospheric conditions, and with the eye shielded from the direct rays of the sun, Venus might be seen as an exceedingly tiny bright point of light. It is possible to see it in daytime when one knows exactly where to look. Of course, the chances of looking at the right spot are very few.

"It has been unofficially reported that the object was a Navy cosmic ray balloon. If this can be established it is to be preferred as an explanation. However, if reports from other localities refer to the same object, any such device must have been a good many miles high - 25 to 50 - in order to have been seen clearly, almost simultaneously, from places 175 miles apart."

This absolutely ruled out the balloon possibility, as the investigator fully realized. That he must have considered the space-ship answer at this point is strongly indicated in the following sentence:

"If all reports were of a single object, in the knowledge of this investigator no man-made object could have been large enough and far enough away for the approximate simultaneous sightings."

The next paragraph of this Project "Saucer" report practically nullified Major Boggs's statement that Venus was the sole explanation:

"It is most unlikely, however, that so many separate persons should at that time have chanced on Venus in the daylight sky. It seems therefore much more probable that more than one object was involved. The sighting might have included two or more balloons (or aircraft) or they might have included Venus (in the fatal chase) and balloons. . .. Such a hypothesis, however, does still necessitate the inclusion of at least two other objects than Venus, and it certainly is coincidental that so many people would have chosen this one day to be confused (to the extent of reporting the matter) by normal airborne objects. . . ."

Farther on in the summaries, I found a report that has an extremely significant bearing on the Mantell case. This was Case 175, in which the same consultant attempts to explain a strange daylight sighting at Santa Fe, New Mexico.

One of the Santa Fe observers described the mysterious aerial object as round and extremely bright, "like a dime in the sky." Here is what the Project "Saucer" investigator had to say:

"The magnitude of Venus was -3.8 (approximately the same as on January 7, 1948). it could have been visible in the daylight sky. It would have appeared, however, more like a pinpoint of brilliant light than 'like a dime in the sky.' It seems unlikely that it would be noticed at all. . . . Considering discrepancies in the two reports, I suggest the moon in a gibbous phase; in daytime this is unusual and most people are not used to it, so that they fail to identify it. While this hypothesis has little to correspond to either report, it is worth mentioning.

"It seems far more probable that some type of balloon was the object in this case."

Both the Godman Field and the Santa Fe cases were

almost identical, so far as the visibility of Venus was concerned. In the Santa Fe case, which had very little publicity, Project "Saucer" dropped the Venus explanation as a practically impossible answer. But in Case 33, it had tried desperately to make Venus loom up as a huge gleaming object during Mantell's fatal chase.

There was only one explanation: Project "Saucer" must have known the truth from the start-that Mantell had pursued a tremendous space ship. That fact alone, if it had exploded in the headlines at that time, might have caused dangerous panic. To make it worse, Captain Mantell had been killed. Even if he had actually died from blacking out while trying to follow the swiftly ascending space ship, few would have believed it. The story would spread like wildfire: Spacemen kill an American Air Force Pilot!

This explained the tight lid that had been clamped down at once on the Mantell case. It was more than a year before that policy had been changed; then the first official discussions of possible space visitors had begun to appear.

True's plans to announce the interplanetary answer would have fitted a program of preparing the people. But the Air Force had not expected such nation-wide reaction from True's article; that much I knew. Evidently, they had not suspected such a detailed analysis of the Godman Field case, in particular. I could see now why Boggs, Jesse Stay, and the others had tried so hard to convince me that we had made a mistake.

It was quite possible that we had revived that first Air

Force fear of dangerous publicity. But Mantell had been dead for two years. News stories would not have the same impact now, even if they did report that spacemen had downed the pilot. And I doubted that there would be headlines. Unless the Air Force supplied some convincing details, the manner of his death would still be speculation.

Apparently I had been right; this case was the key to the riddle. It had been the first major sighting in 1948. Project "Saucer" had been started immediately afterward. In searching for a plausible answer, which could be published if needed, officials had probably set the pattern for handling all other reports, "Explaining away" would be a logical program, until the public could be prepared for an official announcement.

As I went through other case reports, I found increasing evidence to back up this belief.

Case 1, the Muroc Air Base sightings, had plainly baffled Project men seeking a plausible answer. Because of the Air Force witnesses, they could not ignore the reports. Highly trained Air Force test pilots and ground officers had seen two fast-moving silver-colored disks circling over the base.

Flying at speeds of from three to four hundred miles an hour, the disks whirled in amazingly tight maneuvers. Since they were only eight thousand feet above the field, these turns could be clearly seen.

"It is tempting to explain the object as ordinary aircraft observed under unusual light conditions," the case report reads. "But the evidence of tight circles, if maintained, is strongly contradictory."

Although Case 1 was technically in the "unexplained" group, Wright Field had made a final effort to explain away the reports. Said the Air Materiel Command:

"The sightings were the result of misinterpretation of real stimuli, probably research balloons."

In all the world's history, there is no record of a three-hundred-mile-an-hour wind. To cover the distance involved, the drifting balloons would have had to move at this speed, or faster. If a three-hundred-mile wind had been blowing at eight thousand feet, nothing on earth could have stood it, Muroc Air Base would have been blown off the map.

What did the Muroc test pilots really see that day?

While searching for the Chiles-Whitted report, ran across the Fairfield Suisan mystery-light case, which I had learned about in Seattle. This was Case 215. The Project "Saucer" comment reads:

"If the observations were exactly as stated by the witnesses, the ball of light could not be a fireball. . . . A fireball would not have come into view at 1,000 feet and risen to 20,000. If correct, there is no astronomical explanation. Under unusual conditions, a fireball might appear to rise somewhat as a result of perspective. The absence of trail and sound definitely does not favor the meteor hypothesis, but . . . does not rule it out finally. It does not seem likely any meteor or auroral phenomenon could be as bright as this."

Then came one of the most revealing lines in all the case reports:

"In the almost hopeless absence of any other natural explanation, one must consider the possibility of the object's having been a meteor, even though the description does not fit very well."

One air-base officer, I recalled, had insisted that the object had been a lighted balloon. Checking the secret report from the Air Weather Service, I found this:

"Case 2 15. Very high winds, 60-70 miles per hour from southwest, all levels. Definitely prohibits any balloon from southerly motion."

This case is officially listed as answered

In Case 19, where a cigar-shaped object was seen at Dayton, Ohio, the Project investigator made a valiant attempt to fit an answer:

"Possibly a close pair of fireballs, but it seems unlikely. If one were to stretch the description to its very limits and make allowances for untrained observers, he could say that the cigar-like shape might have been illusion caused by rapid motion, and that the bright sunlight might have made both the objects and the trails nearly invisible.

"This investigator does not prefer that interpolation, and it should he resorted to only if all other possible explanations fail."

This case, too, is officially listed as answered

Case 24, which occurred June 12, 1947, twelve days before the Arnold sighting, shows the same determined attempt to find an explanation, no matter how farfetched.

In this case, two fast-moving objects were seen at Weiser, Idaho, Twice they approached the earth, then swiftly circled upward. The Project investigator tried hard to prove that these might have been parts of a double fireball. But at the end, he said, "In spite of all this, this investigator would prefer a terrestrial explanation for the incident."

It was plain that this report had not been planned originally for release to the public. No Project investigator would have been so frank. With each new report, I was more and more convinced that these had been confidential discussions of various possible answers, circulated between Project "Saucer" officials. Why they had been released now was still a puzzle, though I began to see a glimmer of the answer.

The Chiles-Whitted sighting was listed as Case 144. As I started on the report, I wondered if Major Boggs's "bolide" answer would have any more foundation than these other "astronomical" cases.

The report began with these words:

"There is no astronomical explanation, if we accept the report at face value. But the sheer improbability of the facts as stated, particularly in the absence of any known aircraft in the vicinity, makes it necessary to see whether any other explanation, even though farfetched, can be considered."

After this candid admission of his intentions, the Project consultant earnestly attempts to fit the two pilots' space ship description to a slow-moving meteor.

"It will have to be left to the psychologists," he goes on, "to tell us whether the immediate trail of a bright meteor could produce the subjective impression of a ship with lighted windows. Considering only the Chiles-Whitted sighting, the hypothesis seems very improbable."

As I mentioned in an earlier chapter, observers at Robbins Air Force Base, Macon, Georgia, saw the same mysterious object streak overhead, trailing varicolored flames. This was about one hour before Chiles and Whitted saw the onrushing space ship.

To bolster up the meteor theory, the Project consultant suggests a one-hour error in time. The explanation: The airliner would be on daylight-saving time.

"If there is no time difference," he proceeds, "the object must have been an extraordinary meteor. . . . in which case it would have covered the distance from Macon to Montgomery in a minute or two."

Having checked the time angle before, I knew this was incorrect. Both reports were given in eastern standard time. And in a later part of the Project report, the consultant admits this fact. But he has an alternate answer: "If the difference in time is real, the object was some form of known aircraft, regardless of its bizarre nature."

The "bizarre nature" is not specified. Nor does the Project "Saucer" report try to fit the Robbins Field description to any earth-made aircraft. The air-base observers were struck by the object's huge size, its projectile-like shape, and the weird flames trailing behind. Except for the double-deck windows, the air-base men's description tallied with the pilots'. With the ship at five thousand feet or higher, its windows would not have been visible from the ground. All the observers agreed on the object's very high speed.

Neither of the Project "Saucer" alternate answers will fit the facts.

1. The one-hour interval has been proved correct. Therefore, as the Project consultant admits, it could not be a meteor.

2. The Robbins Field witnesses have flatly denied it was a conventional plane. The Air Force screened 225 airplane schedules, and proved there was no such plane in the area. No ordinary aircraft would have caused the brilliant streak that startled the DC-3 passenger and both of the pilots.

Major Boggs's bolide answer had gone the way of his Venus explanation. I wondered if the Gorman light-balloon solution would fade out the same way.

But the Project report on Gorman (Case 172) merely hinted at the balloon answer. In the Appendix, there was a brief comment: "Note that standard 30 inch and 65 inch weather balloons have vertical speeds of 600 and 1100 feet per minute, respectively."

In all the reports I have mentioned, and on through both the case books, one thing was immediately obvious. All the testimony, all the actual evidence was missing. These were only the declared conclusions of Project "Saucer." Whether they matched the actual conclusions in Wright Field secret files there was no way of knowing.

But even in these sketch reports, I found some odd hints, clues to what Project officials might really be thinking.

After an analysis of two Indianapolis cases, one investigator reports:

"Barring hallucination, these two incidents and 17, 75 and 84 seem the most tangible from the standpoint of description, of all those reported, and the most difficult to explain away as sheer nonsense."

Case 17, I found, was that of Kenneth Arnold. But in spite of the above admission that this case cannot be explained away, it is officially listed as answered.

Case 75 struck a familiar note. This was the strange occurrence at Twin Falls, Idaho, on which True had had a tip months before. A disk moving through a canyon at tremendous speed had whipped the treetops as if by a violent hurricane. The report was brief, but one sentence stood out with a startling effect:

"Twin Falls, Idaho, August 13, 1847," the report began. "There is clearly nothing astronomical in this incident. . . . Two points stand out, the sky-blue color, and the fact that the trees 'spun around on top as if they were in a vacuum.'"

Then came the sentence that made me sit up in my chair.

"Apparently it must be classed with the other bona fide disk sightings."

The other bona fide sightings!

Was this a slip? Or had the Air Force deliberately left this report in the file? If they had, what was back of it - what was back of releasing all of these telltale case summaries?

I skimmed through the rest as quickly as possible looking for other clues. Here are a few of the things that. caught my eye:

Case 10. United Airlines report . . . despite conjectures, no logical explanation seems possible. . . .

Case 122. Holloman Air Force Base, April 6, 1948. [This was the Commander McLaughlin White Sands report.] No logical explanation. . .

Case 124. North Atlantic, April 18, 1948 . . . radar sighting . . . no astronomical explanation. . . .

Case 127. Yugoslav-Greek frontier, May 7, 1948 . . . information too limited. . . .

Case 168. Arnheim, The Hague, July 20, 1948 . . . object seen four times . . . had two decks and no wings very high speed comparable to a V-2. . . .

Case 183. Japan, October 15, 1948. Radar experts should determine acceleration rates. . . .

Case 188. Goose Bay, Labrador, October 29, 1948. Not astronomical . . . picked up by radar . . . radar experts should evaluate the sightings . . . .

Case 189. Goose Bay, Labrador, October 31, 1948 . . . not astronomical . . . observed on radarscope. . . .

Case 196. Radarscope observation . . . object traveling directly into the wind. . . .

Case 198. Radar blimp moving at high speed and continuously changing direction. . . .

Case 222. Furstenfeldbruck, Germany, November 23, 1948 . . . object plotted by radar DF at 27,000 feet . . . short time later circling at 40,000 feet . . . speed estimated 200-500 m.p.h. . . .

Case 223 . . . seventeen individuals saw and reported object . . .green flare . . . all commercial and government airfield questioned . . . no success. . . .

Case 224. Las Vegas, New Mexico, December 8, 1948 description exactly as in 223 . . . flare reported traveling very high speed . . . very accurate observation made by two F.B.I. agents. . . .

Case 231 . . . another glowing green flare just as described above. .

Case 233 . . . definitely no balloon . . . made turns . . . accelerated from 200 to 500 miles per hour . . . .

Going back over this group of cases, I made an incredible discovery: All but three of these unsolved cases were officially listed as answered.

The three were the United Airlines case, the White Sands sightings, and the double-decked space-ship report from The Hague.

Going back to the first report, I checked all the summaries. Nine times out of ten, the explanations were pure conjecture. Sometimes no answer was even attempted.

Although 375 cases were mentioned, the summaries ended with Case 244. Several cases were omitted. I found clues to some of these in the secret Air Weather Service report, including the mysterious "green light" sightings at Las Vegas and Albuquerque.

Of the remaining 228 cases, Project "Saucer" lists all but 34 as explained. These unsolved cases are brought up again for a final attempt at explaining them away. In the appendix, the Air Materiel Command carefully states:

"It is not the intent to discredit the character of observers, but each case has undesirable elements and these can't be disregarded."

After this perfunctory gesture, the A.M.C. proceeds to discredit completely the testimony of highly trained Air Force test pilots and officers at Muroc. (The 300-400 m.p.h. research balloon explanation.)

The A.M.C. then brushes off the report of Captain Emil Smith and the crew of a United Airline plane. On July 4, 1947, nine huge flying disks were counted by Captain Smith and his crew. The strange objects were in sight for about twelve minutes; the crew watched them for the entire period and described them in detail later.

Despite Project "Saucer's" admission that it had no answer, the A.M.C. contrived one. Ignoring the evidence of veteran airline pilots, it said:

"Since the sighting occurred at sunset, when illusory effect are most likely, the objects could have been ordinary aircraft, balloons, birds, or pure illusion."

In only three cases did the A.M.C. admit it had no answer. Even here, it was implied that the witnesses were either confused or incompetent.

In its press release of December 27, 1949, the Air Force had mentioned 375 cases. It implied that all of these were answered. The truth was just the reverse, as was proved by these case books. Almost two hundred cases still were shown to be unsolved-although the real answers might be hidden in Wright Field files.

These two black books puzzled me. Why had the Air Force lifted its secrecy on these case summaries? Why had Major Boggs given me those answers, when these books would flatly refute them?

I thought I new the reason now but there was only one way to make sure. The actual Wright Field files should tell the answer.

When I phoned General Sory Smith, his voice sounded a little peculiar. "I called Wright Field," he said. "But they said you wouldn't find anything of value out there."

"You mean they refused to let me see their files?"

"No, I didn't say that. But they're short of personnel. They don't want to take people off other jobs to look up the records."

"I won't need any help," I said. "Major Boggs said each

case had a separate book. If they'd just show me the shelves, I could do the job in two days."

There was a long silence.

"I'll ask them again," the General said finally. "Call me sometime next week."

I said I would, and hung up. The message from Wright Field hadn't surprised me. But Smith's changed manner did. He had sounded oddly disturbed.

While I was waiting for Wright Field's answer, Ken Purdy phoned. He told me that staff men from Time and Life magazines were seriously checking on the "little men" story. Both Purdy and I were sure this was a colossal hoax, but there was just a faint chance that someone had been on the fringe of a real happening and had made up the rest of the story.

They key man in the story seemed to be one George Koehler, of Denver, Colorado. The morning after Purdy called, I took a plane to Denver. During the flight I went over the "little men" story again. It had been printed in over a hundred papers.

According to the usual version, George Koehler had accidentally learned of two crashed saucers at a radar station on our southwest border. The ships were made of some strange metal. The cabin was stationary, placed within a large rotating ring.

Here is the story as it was told in the Kansas City Star:

In flight, the ring revolved at a high rate of speed, while the cabin remained stationary like the center of a gyroscope. Each of the two ships seen by Koehler were occupied by a crew of two. In the badly damaged ship, these bodies were charred so badly that little could be learned from them. The occupants of the other ship, while dead when they were found, were not burned or disfigured, and, when Koehler saw them, were in a perfect state of preservation. Medical reports, according to Koehler, showed that these men were almost identical with earth-dwelling humans, except for a few minor differences. They were of a uniform height of three feet, were uniformly blond, beardless, and their teeth were completely free of fillings or cavities. They did not wear undergarments, but had their bodies taped.

The ships seemed to be magnetically controlled and powered. In addition to a piece of metal, Koehler had a clock or automatic calendar taken from one of the crafts.

Koehler said that the best assumption as to the source of the ships was the planet Venus.

When I arrived at Denver, I went to the radio station where Koehler worked. I told him that if he had proof that we could print, we would buy the story.

As the first substantial proof, I asked to see the piece of strange metal he was supposed to have. Koehler said it had been sent to another city to be analyzed. I asked to see pictures of the crashed saucers. These, too, proved to be somewhere else. So did the queer "space clock" that Koehler was said to have.

By this time I was sure it was all a gag. I had the feeling that Koehler, back of his manner of seeming indignation at my demands, was hugely enjoying himself. I cut the interview short and called Ken Purdy in New York.

"Well, thank God that's laid to rest," he said when I told him.

But even though the "little men" story had turned out - as expected - a dud, Koehler had done me a good turn. An old friend, William E. Barrett, well-known fiction writer, now lived in Denver. Thanks to Koehler's gag, I had a pleasant visit with Bill and his family.

On the trip back, I bought a paper at the Chicago airport. On an inside page I ran across Koehler's name. According to the A.P., he had just admitted the whole thing was a big joke.

But in spite of this, the "little men" story goes on and on. Apparently not even Koehler can stop it now.

CHAPTER XIX

FOR TWO WEEKS after my return to Washington, General Sory Smith held off a final answer about my trip to Wright Field. Meantime, Ken Purdy had called him backing my request to see the Project files.

It was obvious to me that Wright Field was determined not to open the files. But the General was trying to avoid making it official.

"Why can't you accept my word there's nothing to the saucers?" he asked me one day. "You're impeaching my personal veracity."

But finally he saw there was no other way out. He told me I had been officially refused permission to see the Wright Field files. Some time later, Ken Purdy phoned General Smith.

"General, if the Air Force wants to talk to us off the record, we'll play ball. True will either handle it from then on whatever way you think best or we'll keep still."

Whether this offer was relayed higher up, I don't know. But nothing came of it.

Meantime, saucer reports had begun to come in from

all over the country. Some even came from abroad. Some of these 1950 sightings have already been mentioned in early chapters. Besides the strange affair at Tucson on February 1, there were several other cases in February. Three of these were in South America. One saucer was reported near the naval air station at Alameda, California. Some were sighted in Texas, New Mexico, and other parts of the Southwest.

In March, the wave of sightings reached such a height that the Air Force again denied the saucers' existence. This followed a report that a flying disk had crashed near Mexico City and that the wreckage had been viewed by U. S. Air Force officials.

Scores of Orangeburg, South Carolina, residents watched a disk that hovered over that city on March 10. It was described as silver-bright, turning slowly in the air before it disappeared. The day before this, residents of Van Nuys, California, saw a bright disk moving swiftly four hundred feet in the air. Seen through a telescope, it appeared to be fifty feet in diameter.

Disks were reported at numerous places in Mexico, including Guadalajara, Juárez, Mazatlán, and Durango. On the twelfth of March, the crew and passengers of an American Airlines ship saw a large gleaming disk high above Monterrey airport in Mexico.

Captain W. R. Hunt, the senior airline pilot, watched the disk through a theodolite at the airport. This disk and most of the others seen in Mexico were similar in description to the one sighted at Dayton, Ohio, on March 8. This was the large metallic saucer that hovered high over Vandalia Airport, until Air Force and National Guard fighters raced up after it. The disk rose vertically into the sky at incredible speed, hovered a while longer, and then vanished.

Within twenty-four hours this mystery disk had been "identified" as the planet Venus. (It was broad daylight.) Newspapers quoted "trained astronomical officials in Dayton" as the source for this explanation.

Meanwhile the Mexican government newspaper, El Nacional, quoted "a famous and reputable astronomer" as saying the numerous disks reported over Mexico "carry visitors from Mars."

One of the strangest reports came from the naval air station at Dallas, Texas. It was about 11:30 A.M. on March 16 when CPO Charles Lewis saw a disk streak up at a B-36 bomber. The disk appeared about twenty to twenty-five feet in diameter, Lewis reported. Racing at incredible speed, it shot up under the bomber, hung there for a second, then broke away at a 45-degree angle. Following this, it shot straight up into the air and disappeared.

Captain M. A. Nation, C. O. of the station, said it was "I the second report in ten days. On March 7, said Captain Nation, a tower control operator named C. E. Edmundson saw a similar disk flying so fast it was almost a blur.

"He estimated its speed at three thousand to four thousand miles per hour," Captain Nation stated. "Of course, he had no instruments to compute the speed, so that's a pure estimate."

It was some time before this when I heard the first

crazy rumor about the guided-missile display. This story, which had new details every time I heard it described the Air Force as refusing to let the Navy announce a new type of missile. According to the rumors, the Air Force was trying to prove its own missile far superior, to keep the Navy from invading its long-range bombing domain. Then the Army joined the pitched battle with still a third guided missile, according to the rumors.

And the flying disks? Army, Navy, and Air Force missiles, launched in droves all over the country to prove whose was the best? A public missile race, with the joint Chiefs of Staff to decide the winner!

It seems fantastic that this theory would be believed by any intelligent person. In effect, it accuses the armed services of deliberate, criminal negligence, of endangering millions in the cities below.

I am convinced that some of these rumors led to at least one of the published guesses about our missile program. One widely publicized story stated that the flying saucers seen hurtling through our skies are actually two types of secret weapons. One, according to radio and newspaper accounts, is a disk that whizzes through space, halts suspended in the air, soars to thirty thousand feet, drops to one thousand feet, and then usually disintegrates in the air.

These saucers, it was said, ranged from 20 inches to 250 feet in diameter. They were supposed to be pilotless - and harmless.

The second type was said to be a jet version of the Navy's circular airfoil " Flying Flapjack. " It was credited with fantastic speed.

The "true disks," however, were mainly Air Force devices, according to the report.

"Some are guided, others are not," said the radio commentator who released this story. "They can stay stationary, dash off to right or left, and move like lightning. But they are utterly harmless."

In these "harmless" disks there was supposed to be an explosive charge that destroyed them in mid-air at a predetermined time.

Within a few days after this story was broadcast, the United States News and World Report declared that the saucers are real, and identified them as jet models of Navy "Flying Flapjacks." This magazine, which is not an official publication despite its name, mentioned the variable-direction jet principle that I had previously described in the True article.

These two flying-saucer "explanations" brought denials from the White House, the Navy, and the Air Force.

The Air Force flatly declared that:

1. None of the armed forces is conducting secret experiments with disk-shaped flying objects that could be a basis for the reported phenomena.

2. There is no evidence that the latter stem from the activities of any foreign nation.

Before this, President Truman stated he knew nothing

of any such objects being developed by the United States or any other nation.

The Navy denial came immediately after the first broadcast story. It ran:

"The Navy is not engaged in research or in flying any jet-powered, circular-shaped aircraft."

The Navy added that one model of a pancake-shaped aircraft, called the Zimmerman Skimmer, was built but was never flown. However, a small, three-thousand-pound scale model did fly and was under radio control during flight. This last device is now being rumored as the Navy's unpiloted "missile," said to have been launched over the country like the so-called "harmless" disks.

Even though all these accounts have been officially denied, many Americans may still believe they are true. I have no desire to criticize the authors of these stories; I believe that in following up certain guided-missile leads they were misled into accepting the conclusions they gave.

But these stories, particularly the accounts of huge unpiloted disks, may have planted certain fears in the public mind-fears that are completely unwarranted. For this reason, I have personally checked at Washington in regard to the dangers of unpiloted missiles. Here aye the facts I learned:

1. Neither the Army, Navy, nor Air Force has at any time staged any guided-missile competition as rumored.

2. No unpiloted missiles or remote-controlled experimental craft have been tested over American cities or heavily populated areas.

3. No unpiloted missile carrying dangerous explosives, whether for destruction of the device or other purposes, has been deliberately launched or tested over heavily populated areas.

In regard to the so-called jet-propelled "Flying Flapjack," I have been assured by Admiral Calvin Bolster, of the Navy Bureau of Aeronautics, that this type of plane has never been produced. I concede that he might make this statement to conceal a secret development, but there is one fact of which every American can be certain: Neither this type, nor the radio-controlled smaller model, has been or will be flown or launched over areas where people would be endangered.

The three armed services are working on guided missiles. They are not risking American lives by launching such missiles at random across the United States,

Although most of our guided-missile projects are secret, it is possible to give certain facts about guided-missile developments in general.

The first successful long-range missiles were produced by the Germans. These were the buzz-bomb and. the V-2 rocket. But research in various other types was carried on during the war. Some of this was with oval and round types of airfoils. As already stated by Paul Redell, there is strong evidence that the disk-shaped foil resulted from German observations of either space ships or remote-control disk-shaped "observer units." All the Nazi space-exploration plans followed this discovery that we were being observed by a race from another planet.

After the end of World War II, the international guided-missile race began, with the British, Russians, and ourselves as the chief contenders. Numerous types have been developed-winged bombs, small radar-guided projectiles launched from planes, and ground-to-plane plane-to-ground, and plane-to-plane missiles, equipped with target homing devices.

In certain recent types, the range can be stated as several hundred miles. So far as I have learned, after weeks of rechecking this point, not a single long-range missile has been identified as Russian.

Since this country is working closely with Great Britain on global defense problems, it is no violation of security to say that we have probably exchanged certain guided-missile information. In regard to the British long-range missile picture outlined to me by John Steele, I can state two major facts:

1. The British have categorically denied testing such long-range missiles over American territory, where they might endanger American citizens. There is convincing evidence that they are telling the truth.

2. There is no British missile now built, or planned, that could explain the objects seen by Captain Mantell, Chiles and Whitted, and witnesses in most of the major sightings.

The preceding statement applies equally to

American-built missiles. There is no experimental craft or guided missile even remotely considered in this country that would begin to approach the dimensions and performance of the space ships seen in these cases.

There is concrete evidence that the United States is as well advanced as any other nation in guided-missile development. Certain recent advances should place us in the lead, unless confidential reports on Soviet progress are completely wrong.

If American scientists and engineers can learn the source of the space ships' power and adapt it to our use, it may well be the means for ending the threat of war. The Soviet scientists are well aware of this; their research into cosmic rays and other natural forces has been redoubled since the flying-saucer reports of 1947.

The secret of the space ships' power is more important than even the hydrogen bomb. It may someday be the key to the fate of the world.

CHAPTER XX

AFTER one year's investigation of the flying saucers and Air Force operations, I have come to the following conclusions:

1. The Air Force was puzzled, and badly worried when the disks first were sighted in 1947.

2. The Air Force began to suspect the truth soon after Mantell's death - perhaps even before.

3. Project "Saucer" was set up to investigate and at the same time conceal from the public the truth about the saucers.

4. During the spring of 1949 this policy, which had been strictly maintained by Forrestal, underwent an abrupt change. On top-level orders, it was decided to let the facts gradually leak out, in order to prepare the American people.

5. This was the reason for the April 27, 1949, report, with its suggestions about space visitors.

6. While I was preparing the article for the January 1950 issue of True, it had been considered in line with the general education program. But the unexpected public reaction was mistaken by the Air Force for

hysteria, resulting in their hasty denial that the saucers existed.

7. Because the Air Force feared any closer analysis of the Mantell case, Major Boggs was instructed to publicize the Venus explanation. Although it had been denied, the Air Force knew that most people had forgotten this or had never known it.

8. Major Boggs, having stated this answer publicly (along with the other Chiles-Whitted and Gorman answers), was forced to stick to it, though he knew it was wrong and that the case summaries would prove it.

9. The case summaries were released to a small number of Washington newsmen, to continue planting the space-travel thought; this decision being made after True's reception proved to the Air Force that the public was better prepared than had been thought.

In regard to the flying saucers themselves, I believe that in the majority of cases, space ships are the answer:

1. The earth has been under periodic observation from another planet, or other planets, for at least two centuries.

2. This observation suddenly increased in 1947, following, the series of A-bomb explosions begun in 1945.

3. The observation, now intermittent, is part of a long-range survey and will continue indefinitely. No immediate attempt to contact the earth seems evident. There may be some unknown block to making contact,

but it is more probable that the spacemen's plans are not complete.

I believe that the Air Force is still investigating the saucer sightings, either through the Air Materiel Command or some other headquarters. It is possible that some Air Force officials still fear a panic when the truth is officially revealed. In that case, we may continue for a long time to see routine denials alternating with new suggestions of interplanetary travel.

The education problem is complicated by two imperative needs. We must try to learn as much as we can about the space ships' source of power, and at the same time try to prevent clues to this information from reaching an enemy on earth,

If censorship is suddenly imposed on all flying-saucer reports, this will be the chief reason. This would also help solve a minor problem where partial censorship now exists. A few test missiles launched from a southwest base have been seen by citizens at a distance from the proving grounds. In some cases, their reports have got into local papers, though the wire services did not carry them.

These missile tests are peculiarly different from the general run of flying-saucer reports. Contrasted with the Chiles-Whitted, Mantell, and other space-ship sightings, they stand out with a certain pattern, easy to recognize. News or radio reports of these tests might accidentally give an enemy clues to the type, speed, and range of this particular missile, once he learned the pattern. Periodic censorship, or even a complete blackout of sighting reports, may be enforced during the next year or so.

For the purposes mentioned, such action would be justified. But whenever such censorship is lifted, the complete truth about space visitors should be told at the same time: the full details of all the major cases, the size of the Godman Field space ship, any attempted landings or other efforts at contact by interplanetary visitors, and all other details that now are official secrets.

I also believe that a certain group of disk sightings in this country is linked with our guided missiles. Official announcements, of course, may be delayed a long time. With this exception, I believe that Americans should be told the truth, now.

When the announcement of our guided missiles is made , some Americans not familiar with the facts may accept it as a full answer. If officials are not yet ready to reveal the space-travel facts, the Mantell evidence and other key cases may be deliberately glossed over.

But even if all the evidence - the world-wide sightings, the old records, the Chiles-Whitted and other cases - should be completely ignored, Americans cannot escape eventual contact with dwellers on other planets. Even though space visitors never attempt contact with us, sooner or later earthlings will be traveling to distant planets - planets that scientists have said are almost surely inhabited.

The American people have proved their ability to take incredible things. We have survived the stunning impact of the Atomic Age. We should be able to

take the Interplanetary Age, when it comes, without
hysteria.

www.ingramcontent.com/pod-product-compliance
Lightning Source LLC
Chambersburg PA
CBHW020500100426
42813CB00030B/3053/J